poetry: an introduction to its form and art

poetry an introduction

to its form and art

DISCARDED

NORMAN FRIEDMAN
CHARLES A. MC LAUGHLIN

DEPARTMENT OF ENGLISH
UNIVERSITY OF CONNECTICUT

REVISED EDITION

harper & row, publishers
new york, evanston, and london

FOR R. S. CRANE

acknowledgments

"Stopping by Woods," "Desert Places," "Come In," "Revela-
tion," "Design," "Provide, Provide," and "To Earthward," from
Complete Poems of Robert Frost. Copyright, 1930, 1949 by Henry
Holt and Company, Inc. By permission of the publisher.

"Pied Beauty," "The Caged Skylark," "Carrion Comfort," and
"Binsey Poplars," from *Poems of Gerard Manley Hopkins,* Oxford
University Press. By permission of the publisher.

"anyone lived in a pretty how town," copyright 1940 by E. E.
Cummings; "next to of course god america i," copyright 1926 by
Horace Liveright, renewed 1953 by E. E. Cummings; "three
wealthy sisters swore they'd never part," copyright 1950 by E. E.
Cummings. Reprinted from *Poems 1923-1954* by E. E. Cummings.
By permission of Harcourt, Brace and Company, Inc.

"A Refusal to Mourn," "In My Craft or Sullen Art," and "Twenty-
four Years," from *The Collected Poems of Dylan Thomas*. Copyright 1939, 1942, 1946 by New Directions; copyright 1952, 1953
by Dylan Thomas. Reprinted by permission of New Directions
and J. M. Dent & Sons Ltd.

"The Second Coming," "To a Young Girl," "A Coat," "Politics,"
and "Sailing to Byzantium." Reprinted with permission of the
publisher from *Collected Poems* by W. B. Yeats. Copyright 1928
by The Macmillan Company. Renewed 1956 by Georgie Yeats.
By permission of Mrs. Yeats, The Macmillan Company, The
Macmillan Company of Canada, and A. P. Watt & Son.

"The Glass of Water," from *The Collected Poems of Wallace Stevens*. Copyright 1942, 1951, 1954 by Wallace Stevens. By permission of Alfred A. Knopf, Inc.

"Ars Poetica," from *Collected Poems, 1917-1952*, by Archibald MacLeish, Houghton Mifflin Company. By permission of the publisher.

"The Animals," and "The Wayside Station," copyright © 1957 by Edwin Muir. From *Collected Poems, 1921-1951*, by Edwin Muir, Grove Press, Inc. By permission of Grove Press, Inc., and Faber and Faber Ltd.

"A Night in November," "The Darkling Thrush," "Hap," and "The Going," from *Collected Poems of Thomas Hardy*. By permission of The Trustees of the Hardy Estate, The Macmillan Company, and The Macmillan Company of Canada Ltd.

"Spring Strains," "Nantucket," and "The Red Wheelbarrow," from *The Collected Earlier Poems of William Carlos Williams*. Copyright 1938, 1951 by William Carlos Williams. Reprinted by permission of New Directions.

"The Eagle and the Mole," from *Collected Poems*, by Elinor Wylie. Copyright 1932 by Alfred A. Knopf, Inc. By permission of Alfred A. Knopf, Inc.

"Loveliest of Trees," and "Could Man Be Drunk For Ever," from *Complete Poems*, by A. E. Housman. Copyright 1922, © 1959 by Henry Holt and Company, Inc. Copyright 1950 by Barclays Bank, Ltd. By permission of Henry Holt and Company, Inc., The Society of Authors as literary representatives of the Trustees of the Estate of the late A. E. Housman, and Messrs. Jonathan Cape Ltd., publishers of A. E. Housman's *Collected Poems* in England.

"The Journey of the Magi," from *Collected Poems, 1909-1935*, by T. S. Eliot. Copyright 1936 by Harcourt, Brace and Company, Inc. By permission of Harcourt, Brace and Company, Inc., and Faber & Faber Ltd.

"For a Dead Lady," reprinted with the permission of Charles Scribner's Sons from *The Town Down the River*, by Edwin Arlington Robinson. Copyright 1910 by Charles Scribner's Sons; renewal copyright 1938 by Ruth Nivison.

"Here Lies a Lady" and "Dead Boy," from *Selected Poems* by John Crowe Ransom, Vintage Books. Copyright 1924, 1927, 1945 by Alfred A. Knopf, Inc. By permission of Alfred A. Knopf, Inc.

"Women," from *Collected Poems*, by Louise Bogan, The Noonday Press, 1954. By permission of the publisher.

contents

5. ASK WHAT UNIFIES THE CONTEXT   *65*

6. DEFINE THE POEM'S ARTISTIC PURPOSE   *89*

7. ASK HOW THE ARTISTIC PURPOSE IS SERVED BY TECHNIQUE   *115*

8. ASK HOW THE ARTISTIC PURPOSE IS SERVED BY STYLE   *134*

preface to the teacher

Our chief aim in this book has been to make available for college classroom use an approach to poetry which differs in several important respects from the methods of analysis now current in poetry texts. The nature of this approach is taken up at length in Chapters 1 and 2. It will perhaps suffice here to remark that our method shares with the prevailing critical modes a concern for the internal unity of individual poems, but that it differs in its conception of how that unity may be defined. A prominent doctrine of modern poetic theory is that a poem is unified by the balance and reconciliation of opposing attitudes that are manifested through such linguistic devices as irony, paradox, metaphor, and symbol. While not denying the values of such an approach, we shall be more concerned with poems either as portrayals of human experiences, each handled in such a way as to produce a distinctive artistic effect, or as expositions of statements or arguments for rhetorical purposes. Although at first glance this shift in assumption may seem slight, we trust that you will come to appreciate that it has interesting practical consequences. For one thing, we believe that it brings back into view certain aspects of poems and certain differences among them which are usually displaced in current critical discussions, and allows these hitherto neglected elements to contribute to the enjoyment of reading.

Several pedagogic considerations have guided our arrangement of chapters and poems for study. We are convinced that the art of intelligent reading is synonomous with the art of asking intelligent questions. A great handicap among students is that often they do not know what they should want to know, and consequently they read inertly. We have sought, therefore, to explain that one of the things they may come to know is how to understand and appreciate a poem as the product of artistic skill and imagination, to point out the sorts of questions they might ask in pursuing this goal, and to encourage them to apply the questions to poems on their own. The chapters are thus arranged to take up the problems of understanding in the order that they would normally confront the reader of a poem: What do the words mean? In what context are they spoken? How is that context unified? What end is served by the whole? How do the techniques and style contribute to that end? Is the poem good or bad? To illustrate the practical application of the questions appropriate to each level, we return at the end of each of the analytic chapters to Robert Frost's "Desert Places," which is successively analyzed at the level of language, context, and so on.

Each of these seven working chapters is followed by a brief summary of the questions it raises and a group of poems selected for their special appropriateness to those questions. Because we are trying to stimulate the student to ask his own questions, and because we believe the common textbook practice of enveloping poems in clouds of editorial fine print hardly encourages the student to go on after the course to confront poems plain on the page for himself, we have refrained from discussing these poems specifically and from asking individual questions about them. It should be noted that when a new group of poems is approached at the end of a given chapter, the questions raised in the preceding chapters are to be asked as well as those raised within the chapter itself, and that therefore the order of the book is cumulative. It is not until Chapter 9 that any given poem is studied on all levels, and thus the poems appended to earlier chapters are never really used up. By virtue of this arrangement, these earlier poems may be revisited again and again, if time allows, as the class progresses through the book.

In some cases, the poems have been selected so that they form groups of two or three which may profitably be compared and contrasted within the framework of a given chapter. In the case of Chapter 8, they have been arranged chronologically should the instructor wish to develop some observations about period styles and changes in styles. Most of the poems, we trust, are poems of distinction. Some are old favorites, others are less widely read. They represent varying degrees of difficulty, and they embrace a range of authors, periods, styles, and forms.

The book may be adapted to various needs. It fits easily into an introductory course in literary forms which devotes five or six weeks to poetry. In such a course it may be desirable to cover only Chapters 1-6, with the emphasis falling on the analysis of the poems at the end of the chapters. Such matters as these, of course, will depend on the teacher's estimate of the capabilities of his class. We recommend following the sequence of the chapters so that the student may build a notion of poetic forms in a step by step fashion. But there may be reasons for departing from this scheme; logic, alas, is one thing, and persuasion another, and we realize that the requirements of different groups may differ, that the image may be more vivid than the idea. Thus the first and second chapters, which are rather theoretical, may be covered quickly at the beginning of the term and then re-read later, after some or all of Chapters 3-9, which are the working chapters, have been covered. Or, with a group of students who happen to enjoy ideas, more time could be devoted at the outset to the first two chapters. Or, with certain modifications, the chapters, which are units in themselves, could be read in any other order which appears most effective to the instructor. Chapters 5 and 6, however, are the central chapters, figuratively as well as literally, and they should receive as much emphasis as possible.

In a course devoted exclusively to poetry, the slower class should be able to cover all ten chapters thoroughly, while the faster class should be able to branch out—with the help of one of the many inexpensive anthologies available as a supplement—in some of the directions outlined in the Appendix. In more advanced classes devoted to the study of a literary period, in which poetry is either a part or the whole, the book may be used as a supplementary handbook to the material assigned.

NORMAN FRIEDMAN
CHARLES A. McLAUGHLIN

poetry: an introduction to its form and art

1 《《← in quest of poetic form

When the young Elizabethan nobleman, warrior, and poet, Sir Philip Sidney, sat down to defend poetry against the Puritans and practical people of his day, he thought it wise to forewarn his readers of his own enthusiasm for his subject by telling the story of his first riding master, John Pietro Pugliano. It seems that Master Pugliano, not content with merely giving instruction in the art of riding, took every occasion to discourse upon the noble values of horsemanship. "Then would he add certain praises," writes Sir Philip, "by telling what a peerless beast a horse was, the only serviceable courtier without flattery, the beast of most beauty, faithfulness, courage, and such more, that, if I had not been a piece of a logician before I came to him, I think he would have persuaded me to have wished myself a horse."

Although Master Pugliano's affliction—the urge to make oneself important by gilding the subject one teaches—has never seemed to us more natural and forgivable than at this moment when we prepare to set forth our own remarks on poetry, we nevertheless have resolved to remain silent about the noble benefits of that art: how it can sharpen our perceptions of the world about us, how it can enliven and stretch our imaginations, how it can give us moments of pleasure and exaltation, how it can provide truth and wisdom to live by, how it can deepen our sense of humanity, and even how it can sometimes move the world. After all, we prefer to instruct you how to read a poem rather than persuade you to be one. When Sir Philip went to Master Pugliano he wanted above all to know how to handle a horse—which side to mount from, how to hold the reins, how to adjust the length of the stirrups, where to rest his foot in the stirrup, and so on. Similarly we must suppose that what you, as newcomers to poetry, want is to find out what to do with a poem—how to saddle and bridle it and make it your own. After you have learned these skills there will be time enough to count your blessings. Indeed, it is better that you discover these blessings yourself, for how else can you come to believe in all the fine things that are said about poetry?

But if we are primarily concerned with practical instructions for what to do in the presence of Pegasus, we are obliged to say at once that there are many different ways of being practical.

Even though the poem transmits objective signals from outside the reader's mind—that is, its words and sentences, their rhythm and quality, lie open for all to see—and even though there are conventions of varying degrees of objectivity for interpreting the meanings and implications of the language of a poem, it is nevertheless true that the way in which the reader attends to this evidence and organizes it in his mind depends upon something else that *he* brings to the poem. What he brings to the poem, whether he is conscious of it or not, are notions of what poetry is, what he wants to find out about it, and what ways are best for finding it out.

If Master Pugliano will forgive us, a horse may be viewed and consequently approached in a variety of ways. Although a horse is a horse, the veterinarian looks upon him as a physiological system and takes steps to determine whether the parts are properly functioning; the biologist, seeking to assign the horse a place in the animal kingdom, may concern himself with its skeletal structure; the racetrack devotee, interested in running ability, devotes himself to genealogy and the latest racing form; the farmer, looking for an animal which can pull wagons and plows, concerns himself with muscle power; the cow-boy, needing a fast and maneuverable mount, looks for a light and small horse; the pleasure-rider, wanting an attractive and docile animal, seeks a more statuesque variety; or the poet, perhaps searching for a way to describe the force of man's creative imagination, might take the rhythmic power of a running horse as a symbol of his idea.

So, too, poetry may be viewed in various ways and for various purposes, and consequently may call forth various modes of reading on the part of the reader. Our purpose in this book is to set forth an organized approach to one of these modes. In order to clarify this approach, therefore, let us consider some of the major views of poetry that have been held in the past.

Like most things that have interested man over a long period of time, a poem presents a many-sided surface. For one thing, since it comes into being in the midst of a culture, it presents in one degree or another a mirror of the conventions, fashions, tastes, and values of the period in which it was written. When this aspect of poetry seizes the reader's attention, or when he seeks it out, he behaves as a historian. He considers the trustworthiness of the poet as a witness, he extends his inquiry into the poet's other writings, he looks into other types of documents (diaries, journals, newspapers, other forms of art) for confirmation of his findings, and he begins to draw generalizations about the character of the age in question. This aspect of poetry has been widely cultivated in modern times by literary critics such as Edmund Wilson and Lionel Trilling, and by cultural historians such as Spengler and Toynbee, who have often looked to art objects for essential insights into the cultures they study.

Then, too, a poem may bear witness to the poet's outer and inner life—what he saw and did, what his manner of life was, what his qualities of mind and sensibility were, as well as what the structure of his personality was or even what may have been the unconscious feelings of guilt which, according to some schools of psychoanalysis, underlie dreams and poetry alike. This general line of inquiry has a long tradition, extending from Longinus in antiquity to the critical writing of such moderns as T. S. Eliot, Kenneth Burke, and Ernest Jones.

Again, since poetry represents and interprets dramatic images of the human condition, often in its most serious and abiding aspects, or puts forth ideas and doctrines, it can scarcely avoid radiating circles of influence upon the reader's thoughts and conduct. When he looks upon a poem from this point of view, he begins asking questions about the moral implications of the human action represented in the poem, the quality of the agents, and the over-arching views of the poet. He goes on to compare the breadth, complexity, and truth of the vision of life that it portrays with the visions of other poets, and he calculates its possible moral effects upon its readers. As with the other two areas of criticism, here too is found a distinguished line of critics who center their attention upon the relationship of literature to life—Plato, Sidney, Shelley, and Arnold, to name but a few.

There is yet another line of inquiry into which a poem may lead the reader. Aside from its relationship to the age, the personality of the poet, and the realm of moral and philosophical values, a poem exists in its own right as an independent object, having its own form and its own internal relationships. It is not the product of natural laws, as are plants and animals, nor does it come into being merely because of the prevailing temper of the age or because the poet is endowed with special powers of feeling, thought, and imagination. Rather, it comes into being because the poet *makes* it; he applies his special powers to whatever means his mind or his period affords him, all in the service of some end or organizing design sufficiently distinctive to give his poem an identity of its own.

It is this relationship between the poet's design and his choice of means that chiefly concerns us in this book. We want to help you develop the habit of looking upon poems as coming into being through a series of happy inventions, tentative experiments, and delicate choices, all intricately adjusted to the requirements of the whole. A poem, we would insist, is something the poet lives with for a time, consciously guiding and fashioning it in the light of an artistic conception that eventually crystallizes in his imagination. Indeed we would do well to bear in mind R. G. Collingwood's observation, in his *Autobiography*, that as a boy living in a household of artists he "learned to think of a picture not as a finished product exposed for the admiration of virtuosi, but as a visible record, lying about the house, of an attempt to solve a definite problem in painting, so far as the attempt has gone." In short, if we do not push you to the extremity of becoming a poet yourself (we have already given up persuading you to be a poem), at least we aim to start you thinking in the ways a poet thinks when he is at work on a poem. When, in reading a poem, you find yourself asking: why this metaphor? why this beginning point? in what other ways could it have been done? is this the best?—then you can be assured that you are on the right track.

We have chosen to concentrate upon poems as things "made" not because we feel that other inquiries are less interesting or less in need of sound methods of analysis. Rather, we have narrowed our field, first because it is impossible to do everything at once, and second because we believe that the peculiar responsibility of the teacher of literature lies not with biography, history, or moral effects but with the poetic art—an art whose distinctive problems call forth special talents and techniques on the part of the poet and demand special reading skills and understanding on the part of the reader. It is doubtful, of course, whether active reading of poetry can flourish without frequent reference to the poet and his age and to its moral and intellectual influence; surely, good teachers will always wish to keep these multiple aspects of poetry alive in the student's mind. We suggest in the Appendix ways in which these other questions may be handled. Yet it is what the poet *forms* out of his feelings and thoughts and out of the materials supplied by his age that makes him a poet. Also, it is the degree to which the reader attends to this poetic form that makes him a student of poetry rather than a biographer, historian, or moralist. And we may add that the biographer, historian, or moralist who would use poems as evidence is on safer ground if he first understands them as poems.

We have met in the classroom several common objections to this way of viewing poems. How, it is asked, can one be sure that poets have anything to do with artistic designs? And even if they do, how can one be sure what the design is or describe it with any precision? After all, aren't writing and reading poetry subjective matters guided by feeling and intuition, untrammeled by the rigors of fitting means to ends? As for the question of the creative process, it is undoubtedly true that some poets have no notion of what they are doing, and their poems are perhaps best left to the professional probers of the unconscious. However, a large number of poets, if we can believe the testimony of their diaries, letters, and critical writings, as well as the testimony of their poems, do compose with some guiding principle in mind, even if at a given moment they might be sorely pressed to verbalize it. In reading a poem it is best to assume that the poet "knows" somehow what he is doing until it is proven otherwise.

As for the question of recovering the artistic design of a poem, the disagreements over interpretation that arise in class and in the longer and more heated disputes of learned critics would seem to support a skeptical view. We readily agree that it is not always easy to determine the shaping principle of a poem. Sometimes the poet is not sure himself and sometimes his artistic design is so unfamiliar that one cannot grasp it at once. We further agree that, even in the case of clearly organized poems, one never attains mathematical proof that one's interpretation is right. But we do insist that, given a poem whose words and meanings can be understood by all, one interpretation of its organizing principle will come nearer to explaining the artistic choices in the poem than will any alternative interpretation. How to make up one's mind in the face of different interpretations of a poem is one of the indispensable skills for staying aboard the winged horse, and we will give it attention in its proper place.

At this point yet another objection is likely to appear. It may be possible, the student will say, to make an educated guess as to the artistic design of a poem, but doesn't analysis spoil all the fun of reading? In some cases the student means no more than that his own agreeable illusion of what the poem says is shattered by a closer inspection of the text. This charge must be granted, and we can only reply that whatever may be the pleasures of creative reverie, there are at least equal pleasures in attending closely to the poem itself. But even when the student has accurately grasped the feelings, thoughts, or actions of a poem, he sometimes rebels at a closer look, objecting that to turn away from the imaginative experience of the poem to the intellectual problems of ends and means is to erase the immediate emotional effect of the poem. This argument must also be granted. Experiencing and reflecting upon experience are indeed two distinct activities. But it does not follow that, because the first is delightful, the second must be unpleasant. On the contrary, the process of coming to understand the causes of things has pleasures no less intense than those of immediate experience.

And what are these pleasures? We do not believe they are mysterious. If you have ever taken a disinterested pleasure in the pure skill of an athlete, even when he is competing against your own team, or in the precision and elegance of a chess move, or in the functional beauty of an engine design, then you know something of the kind of pleasure we are talking about. It arises fundamentally from an understanding of the problems facing the doer, the thinker, or the maker in his given task, an awareness of the alternatives at his disposal, and finally an appreciation of the appropriateness of his choices in solving his problem. When the solutions are precise, economical, and artful, one is filled with an admiration that rises above envy—an admiration not only for the individual but also for the capacities of our much maligned race.

To point out the way to these pleasures in reading poetry has been our controlling principle in this book and has governed the selection and ordering of our topics. After considering more fully in Chapter 2 the consequences of our assumption that poems are *made*, we set forth in Chapters 3 and 4 the steps by which you may identify and understand the elements that go into the making of a poem. In Chapters 5 through 9 we introduce the principles that are involved in understanding how these elements may be organized into a unified poem, and in Chapter 10 we turn to the crowning skill of winged-horsemanship, the art of making a critical evaluation of a poetic performance. In the Appendix we take up the questions that arise when, after mastering a single poem, you go on to consider it in relationship to all of the poet's writings, to the poetry of the age in which it was written, and to the historical development of the art.

2 ⋘ what form means

Since we have engaged to tell you how to behave in the presence of a poem viewed as something made, it is high time that we laid down our first direction. Here it is: find the *organizing principle* that binds the parts into a whole. However, as wise as this advice may be, it will do you no good until you can recognize an organizing principle when you see one. Since the notion of a unifying conception is the key to everything that we have to say about reading poetry, we shall devote this chapter to making ourselves clear on this matter.

Let us begin with an illustration drawn from a phenomenon that has often interested psychologists—the way the mind goes about organizing visual impressions, particularly when the perceptual clues are not complete. In certain experiments the subject, for example, is presented with cards on which are printed only the partial outlines of familiar objects. The subject perceives what he takes to be merely random markings until suddenly his imagination fills out the suppressed parts of the picture and the senseless markings immediately fall into place as parts of a visual form. This mental set or *gestalt*, which establishes intelligible relations among the separate parts of a picture, offers one illustration of what we mean by an organizing principle.

Another illustration may be provided by the common experience we have all had in suddenly grasping the solution to a problem, whether in math, chess, or the more intellectual parlor games. For example, a problem often cited in logic textbooks to illustrate the nature of logical implication runs as follows:

without resorting to a laborious hand count, how could you prove that there are at a given time at least two trees in the world with the same number of leaves? If this question has never been sprung upon you before, your first response is likely to be puzzlement. You may begin by mulling over at random the information you have about trees and leaves—you recall thinking that in autumn more leaves fall upon your yard than could possibly have hung upon all the trees within the radius of a mile of your home, or you recollect that palm trees have fewer leaves than oaks, that pines do not have leaves, and so on. However, not until you strike upon the fact that the number of trees in the world is greater than the number of leaves that any one tree could possibly have will your mind be flooded with illumination, for it is only then that the resolving insight can be formulated, namely, that when there are more objects to classify than there are categories to contain them, at least one of the categories must have more than one object assigned to it. Here again, then, is an instance of an organizing principle, for it relates the relevant truths about trees and leaves to a general rule of classification in such a way as to resolve the problem.

So far we have considered a perceptual gestalt which synthesized disconnected lines into a visual form, and a logical gestalt which united separate propositions into a chain of logical implication. There is another kind of gestalt, namely, the unifying conception that guides the maker in assembling his materials to achieve his end. Let us consider the simple ax. The inventor of the ax, we must suppose, was looking for a way to reduce trees into manageable pieces of wood, but this purpose was not sufficient to give him the idea of an ax. Necessity is at best only the grandmother of invention. What he needed more immediately was an organizing idea, and he found it in the conception of a wedge affixed to a lever—the wedge adapted to cut through wood and the lever adjusted to the swing of his arms. Once this gestalt-like image or controlling design was formed in the maker's mind, he could then work out the details of his ax. The size and angle of the cutting-edge, the weight of the wedge, and the length and shape of the haft had to be adjusted to permit each ax stroke to be as efficient as possible, and in turn, the materials of the wedge and the haft had to be selected in accordance with the purpose and shape of the ax.

The notion of an organizing principle as it applies to the making of an ax is perhaps already sufficiently obvious, but in order to aid the transfer of that notion to the making of a poem we offer a few further observations. For one thing, let us identify the separable elements that are fused together in the organizing conception of an ax. First of all, of course, is the capacity or power that the ax is to be endowed with, namely, the ability to slice through the fibers of wood. Then there are the parts of the ax which unite to give it this capacity: (1) the shape of its cutting wedge; (2) the manner provided for putting the wedge in action most efficiently, the haft; and (3) the kind of materials of which the wedge and haft are made. These are the necessary components of the whole. If you were to take away any one of them—the power of cutting, the shape, the manner, or the material—or if you were to make a bad choice in handling any one of them, there would be no true and proper ax.

It is also worth observing that in even so simple a tool as an ax the components exist in delicate degrees of adjustment to one another, so that choices about one of the components determine or are determined by choices about the others. In a situation where the handling of one component is so related to the handling of all the others, a hierarchy of choices is established in the making of a successful whole. In the case of the ax, the necessity of slicing through wood (purpose) determines the shape of the wedge, because without knowing what he was trying to accomplish the maker of the ax would have no idea as to what sort of shape he should construct. The purpose of the ax and its shape determine in turn the method chosen for increasing the slicing powers of the wedge (manner), because unless he knows what he is trying to accomplish and by means of what sort of shape the maker of the ax will have no idea how to make the latter most efficiently achieve the former. The combined requirements of purpose, shape, and manner determine the kind of materials best suited for an ax, for unless he knows he is going to slice through wood by means of a wedge affixed to a haft, the maker of the ax will not be able to decide that the wedge must be made of some material harder than wood and capable of holding a cutting edge, and that the haft must be made of some lighter material but of sufficient strength to hold up under the pressures of chopping wood.

A gestalt as to the form of an ax would consist, then, in realizing what the parts are and how they are related: the need to slice through wood calls for a wedge, this combination of means and end calls for a haft to deliver the striking force required, and this combination of means and end and manner calls for steel for the wedge and wood for the haft. *End* governs *shape*, end and shape govern *manner*, and end and shape and manner govern the *materials*. And so it is with any made thing which is a whole.

With this prologue of homely examples and illustrations behind us, let us now at long last bring poetry upon the stage and consider how the concept of an organizing principle operates in the making of a poem. To make all this as vivid as possible we shall undertake to make a poem before your very eyes. If this poem happens to turn out to be one you have read elsewhere over the signature of a certain well-known poet, do not be alarmed. We know only too well that we did not create this poem. We do hope, however, that we shall manage to uncover some of the poetic thinking that must have entered into its creation.

As with the inventor of the ax, the poet is a man in search of an organizing conception—some sudden glimpse of a principle that will allow him to catch in language (which corresponds with the steel and wood of the ax) some human situation or idea (which corresponds with the shape of the wedge) told in such a way (which corresponds with the idea of the haft) as to endow his poem with certain powers of moving our emotions (which correspond with the cutting capacity of the ax). Now just how the poet hits upon his unifying principle—his poetic gestalt, as it were—we cannot tell, nor can the poet. The process that leads him to the insight may start from any point of the compass. He may begin with a certain effect in mind but without a clear notion of the means to be used. Or he may start with a personal experience or an idea without yet being sure of what way he wants to use it. Or, again, he may have at the outset a rhythm or a combination of words and his problem is to find a purpose and a form to match it. But whatever cogitations, reveries, and plumbings of the unconscious lead up to the moment of inspiration, the formal history of the poem does not begin until the organizing principle asserts itself, whether in dazzling detail or only in dim outline to be worked out by more conscious processes.

Suppose we have been musing upon the hypnotic fascination of a certain winter landscape. It is night and snow is falling silently out of the dark sky upon shadowy woods. Whether this image arose from our own memories of snow-fall, or whether we heard or read of such a scene described by others, or whether we imagined it out of whole cloth is not important. What is important is that we want to make something of it and that our pen is motionless until some governing conception springs into our mind. Shall we concentrate upon straight description, seeking to induce in the reader, by vivid and suggestive detail, the hypnotic quality of the scene? Or shall we place an observer on the scene and attempt to arouse in the reader sympathetic feelings by dwelling upon our observer's emotional response to the falling snow? Or, again, shall we try to produce in the reader the impression of a thoughtful man by focusing upon an appropriate chain of reflection invoked in his mind by the mysterious scene? As you can see, the possibilities come thick and fast. The winter landscape is an amorphous thing and may be developed in a variety of ways. At this point our choice among these possibilities will not be an artistically determined one, for no one of them is inherently better than the others. Rather our choice will depend simply on what strikes us as new and interesting.

Suppose, then, after such musings, we suddenly realize that what interests us is the temptation such a scene offers to a man momentarily weary of the incessant pressures of a responsible life. Here is the possibility of a little dramatic vignette. We will show a man coming under the spell of these snowy woods, being momentarily tempted to throw aside all of his earthly ties, and then, with an effort of will, shaking himself free of his brief hallucination to resume his normal ways—all for the sake of arousing in the reader a fitting degree of sympathy and even admiration for this quiet little act of nobility. There, for good or ill, is our organizing conception and our problem as poets is to work out the incident and portray it in such a way as to make it intelligible and to make as vivid as possible its capacity to arouse the effects we are after.

First of all, let us consider the elements of the dramatic incident itself, independent of the manner in which we might portray it. What are the essential phases of our vignette, the irreducible minimum which will make it intelligible and moving? Clearly, there are two: one phase is the emergence of the temptation, and the other is the decision to put it by. If we do not show our hero in the process of being tempted our reader will neither understand nor sympathize with the incident, and unless we show the speaker deciding to resist that temptation our reader will not feel admiration. Thus has our purpose helped determine in our minds what shape our incident should take. What kind of man should our hero be? Two traits relevant to the experience would, of course, be a quiet sense of responsibility that could lead him to an immersion in the round of daily affairs and duties, and an imagination that could occasionally startle him from that round. We need to strike a balance between these opposing motivations. If he were too prosaic the wintry scene would mean nothing to him and our reader would have no sympathy for him. If he were too sensitive, a Keats or Shelley, for example, we would lose the dramatic point of our vignette—the responsible man undergoing a momentary temptation. In short our hero ought to be a man like most men—sane, dutiful, absorbed in the daily round, yet occasionally sensitive to the undertow of mysterious beauty pulling him from his accustomed round.

Apart from deciding what the basic elements of the incident are and what type of character best serves our purpose, we must, of course, get him on the scene. Strolling at midnight? Gazing from a window? Driving by in a car? Since we want to emphasize the intrusion of beauty upon a mind caught up in the normal routine, we ought to avoid strolling and window watching. Rather our hero ought to be going somewhere with a purpose, but preferably not in a car. The speed, the closed windows, the throbbing motor would shut out the fascination of the softly falling snow. All right, then, why not have him riding along in a horse-drawn sleigh coming home, say, from some business in a nearby village?

Having worked out the elements of our dramatic scene, we must now decide upon the manner in which these things may best be put into the poem to bring out our desired effects. Since present actions affect readers most vividly, and since we want to show our reader a man being tempted, the force of that experience will be greatest if we put the scene in the present and show our speaker thinking and feeling as he undergoes the experience directly. The important thing is what goes on inside our hero, and we should therefore allow him to reveal the incident himself. Now where should the poem begin? Since we decided that the first essential phase of the action was the emergence of the temptation, the most direct opening would reveal our protagonist just at the moment that the cause of the temptation (the snowy woods) begins to work upon him. On the principle that economy of means is as desirable in art as in many other matters, we must ask whether there is any need to begin the poem before that point. Should we show him starting out from the village? Should we describe his background, the route he was taking, the thoughts he was having along the way? Our answer is no. Such details are not necessary to render the experience more intelligible, and they might even obscure its essential unity. To start the poem at the point when the protagonist was already deeply attracted by the woods, on the other hand, would run the risk of making his behavior improbable. So let us begin:

Whose woods these are I think I know.

Once we are under way, the two phases of the incident—the temptation and the denial—can follow their natural temporal order. Of these parts, the first is the one that will need the most "doing," for woods do not automatically attract an observer into a mood of surrender. We will have to show the initial state of mind of the hero, the stimulus operating upon him, and the steps by which he is led to feel the full attraction of the woods as a siren call to surrender. The denial can be handled more briefly, for it involves no more than a sudden breaking of the trance.

Now what of the actual wording of the poem? Since our protagonist is speaking to himself as he undergoes the experience, and since all the reader will know about the experience comes from him, we must be careful to choose our words so that they will seem appropriate to the temperament and character of the man as we have conceived him—a sensible, matter-of-fact man, given to exact observation and understatement, and yet graced with imagination. For this we will adopt a straightforward and unadorned manner of expression, relying upon the suggestiveness of certain simple phrases rather than the explicitness of ornate description. Moreover, we ought to vary the quality of the language so as to reflect our hero's shift in mood. In our choice of stanza and rhyme scheme, suppose we take a gamble and try to catch something of the hypnotic power of the scene by employing a rhythmic four-beat line along with an intricately-linked rhyme pattern of almost incantatory quality: aaba, bbcb, ccdc, dddd.

Now at last our organizing conception has been given a local habitation and a name. In stanza one we bring our hero in contact with the woods, but we imply his mundane state of mind by having him see them at first merely as private property and by having him still thinking of the village.

> Whose woods these are I think I know.
> His house is in the village though;
> He will not see me stopping here
> To watch his woods fill up with snow.

In this stanza we have introduced in our hero a note of self-conscious awareness of his momentary isolation from the world of men, who do not see him stopping. In the beginning of stanza two we shall heighten that awareness by making our hero realize that even his horse, unlike himself, is anxious to follow the daily routine:

> My little horse must think it queer
> To stop without a farmhouse near . . .

In this moment of self-conscious isolation, our speaker begins to
look more closely at the scene around him:

> Between the woods and frozen lake
> The darkest evening of the year.

He now awakens more fully to the immediate sensuous quality
of the scene, which we will try to suggest by the very sound of
our language:

> He gives his harness bells a shake
> To ask if there is some mistake.
> The only other sound's the sweep
> Of easy wind and downy flake.

Now that we have brought him to a point where the sensuous
details of the scene can exert their maximum effect, we can have
our speaker suddenly feel the temptation that it offers. He no
longer sees the woods as property or even as particular woods;
rather they are seen as a symbol of escape into the easeful nothingness of death, as is suggested by our use of indeterminate
adjectives (which might equally well apply to the sleep of
death):

> The woods are lovely, dark and deep.

At this moment of greatest temptation, which we keep in proportion by never stating it overtly, the speaker makes his choice,
and this choice too is kept in proportion by our rendering it
through the indirection of the repeated final lines in which we
try to exploit the figurative connotations of sleep as an analogy
of death:

> But I have promises to keep,
> And miles to go before I sleep,
> And miles to go before I sleep.

It would be ridiculous for us to imagine that our "making"
of this poem which you may have recognized by now as Robert

Frost's "Stopping by Woods on a Snowy Evening," in any way resembles the actual steps by which the poet composed it. On the one hand, we did not begin to touch upon the many delicate factors that he had to balance in his mind in choosing first one word and then another. On the other hand, we perhaps posed as conscious problems of artistic choice things that may well have come unbidden to the poet. He may have felt they were right without consciously reasoning why. Moreover, it is not likely that in the actual writing Robert Frost sat down at his desk with his organizing conception clearly in mind and then rigorously deduced the means he would need to carry it out. All that we claim is that at some point along the line he in some way sensed a unifying principle such as we have described and that this principle made all the difference in choosing what was right or wrong for the poem.

With all due apologies to Robert Frost, then, the moral of our chapter remains the same: that to make something, you must first have an end somehow in view and, second, you must catch hold of an insight that will enable you to relate your material, shape, and manner to the attainment of that end.

If the making of a poem may be seen in this light, and if this is the way in which a gestalt works for the poet, then there is some hope that the reader may grasp the same gestalt by working backwards from the finished product to the principles according to which it must have been made. It is to that re-thinking process which we now turn.

First of all, you must understand what the words in the poem mean and what these meanings add up to before you can attempt formal analysis, for the only evidence that you have in making formal theories is to be found in the words of the poem and what they say and imply. Interpretation of meanings, therefore, should precede your search for artistic principles, because it is these meanings which serve as evidence upon which theories are constructed. You must first observe the laws of grammar and the general conventions of interpretation before attempting to frame theories, or else a preconceived theory may distort your sense of what is actually said in the poem.

All of this, including interpreting meanings, involves a process of *inferential reasoning*, and we hope that this process will become more and more clear as the book proceeds. Chapters 4 and 5 sketch out a few of the fundamentals explicitly, so it will be enough here for us to indicate that man's mind has the power to infer what is not known on the basis of relating what is known to certain principles, and that this power may be sharpened by practice.

3 ⫷⫷⫷⫷ begin with the words

In the beginning are the words of the poem—the sole gateway
to the world that the poet makes. Line by line they form themselves into phrases and sentences, the sentences unite to complete the utterance of the speaker, until that world lies at last
revealed. Unfortunately for the cause of poetry, the student
too often finds himself ensnared in words at the very outset of
his adventure, and what was intended as a gateway becomes for
him a roadblock. Indeed, after several such frustrating experiences, he is only too likely to believe that all of the poet's
efforts to speak with distinction, to vivify, to stir up echoes, to
shape a worn language into a new and living utterance are no
more than devilish stratagems to keep him out. This attitude has
become so widespread that one often hears students defining
poetry as writing that is hard to understand.

Consider what is involved in trying to understand what someone says or writes. You take in his words and their relationships and you translate them in your mind into ideas, images,
and feelings. You read "cat," for example, and think of a particular kind of animal. You read "the cat bit the dog" and you
think of a particular kind of action involving this animal and
another one. You read "the dog bit the cat" and you "see" in
your mind a different action involving these animals. The point
is, of course, that words and their relationships are *signs* of
ideas, images, actions, and feelings, and that you must infer
these things from those signs. Certain signs, that is, stand for
certain *meanings*.

The way language functions in the art of poetry may be

clarified by contrasting poetry with music or painting. When an artist paints a picture, you can see his picture directly; to a lesser degree this is true also of music, for when you hear what a composer wrote being played by musicians you hear it directly. Of course, the musicians are reading from a score and in this sense music resembles literature. But literature is different from either painting or music since, even if you hear someone read a poem, you still have to translate signs into meanings. The poem does not "exist" on the page or in the speech of one who recites it, as the painting exists on the canvas or the music exists in the performance of musicians. Only the words and their relationships exist on the page or in the recitation, and the poem comes into being (as far as the reader is concerned) only as the process of making inferences from signs gets underway.

Hence, coming to understand the language of a poem involves hypothetical reasoning, as do all the analytical skills covered in this book, and we now turn to the relevant distinctions and principles upon which we can base sound hypotheses as to a poem's meaning. These principles are not peculiar to poetry; they apply to the interpretation of language wherever it may be found. We understand language according to our experience and our vocabulary, our ability to use dictionaries and reference works, our knowledge and sense of grammar and syntax, our ability to comprehend ideas, our knowledge of the subject of the discourse, our sense of linguistic contexts (the way larger meanings evolve out of smaller ones, the way meanings interact), and so on.

Unfortunately there are no short cuts, no magic formulas, no "Open Sesames." Inevitably the mind must be brought into play, and our suggestions must be limited to pointing out ways of making the process of thought as efficient as possible. We do, however, offer the consolation that with practice the skills of interpreting poetic language tend to become automatic, and reading problems that threatened to swamp the once unpracticed reader no longer even rise to the threshold of consciousness. They are solved by habit just as the once awkward tennis stroke becomes an automatic response with patient practice. But before that happy state can come about, you must plunge into the hard work of self-conscious reading.

What is the student to do when a poem lies before him, mysterious and unyielding? Our answer is easy to state, if not always easy to carry out: locate as specifically as you can the source of the difficulty. Just what is it in the poem that you do not understand? As in any problem-solving situation, the battle is half won when you can state as accurately as possible the question bothering you. Our suggestions, then, will be designed first of all to help you in the art of diagnosing obstructions to understanding.

I

The most obvious stumbling block, of course, is the individual words. One scarcely needs a textbook to remind him that strange and unfamiliar words are trouble spots, and that the remedy lies in repeated visits to a good dictionary. A poem by Gerard Manley Hopkins, entitled "Pied Beauty," begins:

> Glory be to God for dappled things—
> For skies of couple-colour as a brinded cow; . . .

Not many readers would know offhand the meaning of "brinded." The dictionary says the word is an archaic form of "brindled," and that this means having dark streaks or spots on a gray or tawny ground. How this relates to skies of couple-color should be clear enough, but we will discuss the mechanism of this sort of expression in due course.

Less obvious difficulties may arise from the fact that a familiar word often has more than one meaning. The dictionary, for example, says that the word "bar" can be taken in a variety of senses: a length of metal, a conventional sign for writing out music, a ridge of sand formed by river and tidal currents, a tavern, and so on. In reading the lines—

> And may there be no moaning of the bar,
> When I put out to sea . . .

from Alfred, Lord Tennyson's "Crossing the Bar," the inexperienced reader might pause to consider how to take "bar." We once heard a student recite these lines as "May there be no moaning *at* the bar." Becoming suspicious, we asked him how he interpreted the passage, and he replied that he had visions of the speaker's friends gathered at the local tavern to mourn his death. The proper meaning of the term is, of course, conveyed in the poem by the choice of preposition and by the reference in the following line to the sea. In most cases the context directs us to the intended meaning of *ambiguous* words.

Occasionally, however, the poet may choose deliberately to exploit the ambiguity of a word, and here the problem is, first, to recognize that intention, and, second, to decide which possibilities of all the alternative meanings are most suitable. The word "mean" for example, can serve as a verb (to signify), or as an adjective applying to something that is common or shabby, or to a person who is selfish and cruel, or to that which stands between two extremes. Which of these possibilities seems to fit Hopkins' use of the term in "The Caged Skylark"?

Man's mounting spirit in his bone-house, mean house, dwells—

Clearly, almost all of the senses of the term, except the first, apply here: man's flesh is perishable, subject to terrible appetites and discomforts, and hence is humble, shabby, selfish, and in a middle position between heaven and earth.

Or a word may be familiar enough but used by the poet in a special way:

anyone lived in a pretty how town

This line is characteristic of its author, E. E. Cummings, because it involves a *grammatical shift*, using a pronoun as a person's name. The poem is about a man and a woman in love surrounded by a materialistic and loveless society, and Cummings contrasts the qualities of his lovers with the qualities of the society by calling his hero "anyone," his heroine "noone," and society "everyone" and "someone." A twist of meaning is also involved here, because if society thinks of lovers as unimportant, and if Cummings apparently accepts that judgment in his naming of characters, it is nevertheless implied that he really thinks of the lovers as more important. In this case, then, the real sense of the word is in opposition to its apparent sense. Here, as before, the context is the guide.

Even when the individual words are clear, understanding may be blocked by our inability to grasp the relationships among words in phrases, clauses, and sentences. The first job, when this happens, is to locate the subject, the verb, the object, the modifiers, and so on—in short, to grasp the *syntactical structure*. Here is the first stanza of Hopkins's "The Caged Skylark":

As a dare-gale skylark scanted in a dull cage
    Man's mounting spirit in his bone-house, mean house, dwells—
    That bird beyond the remembering his free fells;
This in drudgery, day-labouring-out life's age.

In the opening two lines "spirit" is the subject and "dwells" is the verb of the main clause, and "skylark" and "scanted" the subject and verb of the dependent clause. It is important to recognize from these grammatical clues that the thing talked about in the poem is man's spirit and that the skylark is brought in subordinately as an analogy to help explain man's condition. Since man's spirit has been likened to a skylark, a further problem in this passage is to sort out the two birds referred to at the beginning of lines three and four. Again we must appeal to the context. "That bird," because it once knew what the skylark knew—free fells—takes the skylark as its antecedent, while the "This" of line four, because it has a predicate describing a human condition, takes man's spirit as its antecedent. Moreover the sequence of ideas offers a clue. Line three balances line one, and line four balances line two.

Another difficulty in reading may arise not because the connections among words are obscure but because some of the words are left out. The last stanza of this same poem offers a good illustration in the phrase "at best":

> Man's spirit will be flesh-bound when found at best,
> But uncumbered: . . .

When is man "at best"? When he is young and active? Old and wise? It is only when we recall that the poem was written from the point of view of a Jesuit priest that we realize that this phrase is a very condensed way of saying "at that time when man is resurrected in heaven."

But even when you have translated the language into its proper train of ideas, a further possibility of confusion awaits you. The thoughts themselves may seem strange or even contradictory. The lines just quoted offer examples of this type of difficulty. For persons unfamiliar with Catholic doctrines, the idea that the resurrected soul will be clothed in its body ("flesh-bound") will seem strange. Again the reader will have to recall that the poem was written within the framework of a certain point of view. It may be said that Hopkins *alludes*, in these lines, to the Catholic doctrine of resurrection. We ought to warn you that poets frequently take for granted that their readers know

certain things about myths, stories, theories, doctrines, and so
on. Your job, when confronted with such demanding compli-
ments, is to find out what you don't know; there's no help for
it. A certain amount of knowledge is necessary for reading
poetry, so develop the habit of checking not only dictionaries
but other reference works as well.

But even after this *allusion* is clarified a contradiction still
seems to remain: why, the reader may ask, if the spirit is flesh-
bound on the Day of Judgment, is it "uncumbered"? Again we
must refer to Catholic doctrine. The flesh is mortal, but it will
be made immortal by means of a divine miracle. What in life
was a cage of the spirit will then be in resurrection one of its
glories. To suggest the relationship of soul and body in afterlife Hopkins goes on to draw an analogy:

> . . . meadow-down is not distressed
> For a rainbow footing it nor he for his bónes rísen.

The use of *analogy* or *comparison* opens up another possible
area of difficulty for the inexperienced reader of poetry. He
may not recognize that a comparison is being used; he may
recognize that two things are being compared but confuse the
main subject and what is used for illustration; or he may not
understand the *grounds of likeness* between the *subject* and its
analogue. Although there is no automatic way of resolving the
problems posed by analogies, it is helpful to raise the questions
just suggested in order to narrow the point at issue. In the
lines just quoted from Hopkins it is clear enough from the
grammatical signs that a rainbow-spangled meadow is being
compared with the risen soul and body of man. Since the comparison involves several terms, it is important to consider more
closely what goes with what—the rainbow is to the meadow-
down as the body is to the soul. Given the preceding lines of
the poem, it is clear, of course, that the subject under discus-

sion is man and that the rainbow and the meadow, therefore, serve as the analogue. But what is the ground of likeness between the subject and the analogue? It lies in the fact that neither the rainbow nor the body distress the object with which it is in contact. Indeed, not only is meadow-down not distressed when a rainbow is seen resting upon it, it is positively enhanced. It is just that Hopkins chooses to say less than he really means, and the reader will not fully grasp the point unless he appreciates the existence of this *understatement*.

Unfamiliar words, words of several meanings, words ambiguously used, familiar words used in unfamiliar ways, words used in opposition to their apparent sense, syntactical obscurity, words left out, difficult ideas, allusions, apparent contradictions, comparisons, understatements—all these may raise problems of understanding and require special attention, particularly when they begin to pile up in the same brief passage. Our list does not exhaust all the trouble spots you may run into; the dozen or so we have mentioned simply represent the most common. Each poet has his own characteristic difficulties which require special analysis. Our general advice is that you should never cease asking yourself whether you understand the language of the poem and that, when you have difficulty, you should always attempt to isolate the precise trouble spot.

We should add one further word of caution. So far, we have sought to resolve problems of meaning by referring to the conventions and rules of language. In some cases, however, they are not precise enough to determine the exact meaning of a passage, and we must go beyond the merely linguistic context to the circumstances surrounding the utterance, a matter which will be taken up in the next chapter. It is sometimes necessary to work from some of the important words to the circumstances of the utterance and then, in the light of these circumstances, to return to explain ambiguous passages.

II

Since we have chosen Robert Frost's "Desert Places" as a model to illustrate our discussion throughout this book, we shall begin here with a grammatical reading of this poem.* Although it does not present the difficulties that many poems do, there will be some value in pointing out the care that one must take even with such a relatively clear poem.

DESERT PLACES

Snow falling and night falling fast oh fast
In a field I looked into going past,
And the ground almost covered smooth in snow,
But a few weeds and stubble showing last.

The woods around it have it—it is theirs.
All animals are smothered in their lairs.
I am too absent-spirited to count;
The loneliness includes me unawares.

And lonely as it is, that loneliness
Will be more lonely ere it will be less—
A blanker whiteness of benighted snow
With no expression, nothing to express.

They cannot scare me with their empty spaces
Between stars—on stars where no human race is.
I have it in me so much nearer home
To scare myself with my own desert places.

As far as the words in this poem are concerned, there probably are not many whose meanings you do not already know. It is just possible that one or two readers might have to check

---

* To make it easier to refer to the poem while studying the discussions throughout the book, it has been reprinted on the fold-out sheet following page 181. The two other poems used as models are also reprinted there.

in the dictionary for "lairs," "ere," or "benighted," and if so, they should not be ashamed. There are, however, several other types of difficulty, and we shall take them up line by line.

The three uses of "it" in line five may offer some trouble: what are the woods around? what is theirs? and, indeed, to what or to whom does "theirs" refer? "It" is a third-person singular pronoun and the only singular nouns which precede it are "snow," "night," "field," and "ground." Which of these could the woods be "around?" "Field" is the most likely prospect, since the field was the central topic of the preceding stanza. "Snow," "night," and "ground" occur only as subordinate details in relation to the field. "Theirs" is third-person plural and its antecedent can be established as "woods" on the general principle that a pronoun usually refers back to the nearest preceding noun of the same number. But even when the syntax is clear, you might still wonder about the phrase "have it." It is clear enough that in this case the amorphous "have" implies a notion of ownership, but how can woods "own" anything? Reflection ought to make you aware that Frost is suggesting a *personification:* like some dark power with a will of its own, the woods have reclaimed back into a state of unordered nature the land man had sought to wrest from it.

The next line helps to clear up this point and it throws some light on the following two lines: all signs of life are gone. The meaning of the title also begins to come into play, for the speaker sees this scene as "deserted," devoid of plants and animals. But why is he "too absent-spirited to count"? and what does "absent-spirited" mean, anyhow? "Absent-minded" is a common enough expression (we have even seen a textbook which had this as a misprint in the poem), and it is likely that Frost was aiming at freshness of expression by giving the term a new twist. By analogy "absent-spirited" seems to mean that his "spirit" (or soul, or life-principle, or consciousness) is not

functioning properly; it is forgetful, heedless. He doesn't
"count" in the sense that, although he is the only living thing
in sight, he really isn't wholly alive either.

The eighth line also presents a difficulty. How is the common
word "unawares" to be taken in this context? The dictionary
says that it is an adverb. Consequently it must modify the verb
"includes." The seventh and eighth lines can be paraphrased as
follows: "Since I'm not really alive enough to count as an ex-
ception to the pervading desolation, the dark power of the
woods (Frost is continuing the personification established earlier) swallows me up without even noticing me."

Why, in the third stanza, will that loneliness be more before
it will be less? Well, in the first stanza it was clear that the
snow and the night were responsible for the desolation of the
scene. The inference, then, is simply that snowfall and nightfall
are just beginning and that they will deepen before they are
through. The syntax of the next two lines is clear enough, but
perhaps the idea involved needs some elucidation. In what sense
could the scene *have* an "expression," so that the poet may say
that now it has none? The snow and the night are reducing, as
is evident by now, the scene to a gloomy white anonymity: the
trees are bare of leaves, the weeds and stubble are being
smothered, the animals are not in sight, the speaker is too
absent-spirited to count, and there's just nothing there at all,
as in a desert. On the other hand, during (say) spring everything alive would be in sight, would be growing, and therefore
would reassure a sensitive observer that there was some purpose
in the world. Thus, the inference is that since no signs of life are
evident to the speaker, it appears that there is no purpose, no
meaning, "nothing to express."

To whom does "They" refer at the opening of the last
stanza? Certainly there is no antecedent in the preceding lines
that would have the power to scare the speaker with empty

places between the stars. Who, then, does have this power? Frost is no doubt alluding to the modern scientists who have offered, in place of a meaningful, God-centered world, a vast and empty universe under the dominion of indifferent natural law.

The final trouble spot is to be found in the last line in the phrase "my own desert places." The reader must recognize that an implied comparison is involved here. That is, the desert places in the realm of nature—the snowy field and the empty spaces between stars—are being compared to something within man. What frightening, desert places might a man have within himself? Perhaps a sense of his own purposelessness or of his own moral and spiritual failings. This desolation is far more frightening than that presented by the realm of nature, for there is no escape from it (it is "nearer home," which doesn't appear to mean, as some students would have it, the speaker's actual "house"), and, moreover, it is, in a sense, the desert within man that makes the world of nature seem a desert to him.

With these suggestions as to how the words of a poem may be understood, the first stage in the reading of "Desert Places" is now completed, and we are ready to move on to the next— defining the context in terms of which the words are spoken.

poems for study and discussion

The following poems have been chosen because they offer rather more difficulty in understanding than usual. Your problem is to make sure you grasp the meaning of all the words, phrases, clauses, sentences, allusions, comparisons, ideas, and so on, in the poems assigned. A useful practice is to write out paraphrases of difficult passages, as we have done, or even of whole poems. Naturally you should not assume that such paraphrases, because they are more easily understood, are better than the original, for poets aim at special effects by their use of language and it is these effects (to be studied later) which are lost in a paraphrase.

PIED BEAUTY ⋘ *Gerard Manley Hopkins*

Glory be to God for dappled things—
  For skies of couple-colour as a brinded cow;
    For rose-moles all in stipple upon trout that swim;
Fresh-firecoal chestnut-falls; finches' wings;
  Landscape plotted and pieced—fold, fallow, and plough;
    And áll trádes, their gear and tackle and trim.

All things counter, original, spare, strange;
  Whatever is fickle, freckled (who knows how?)
    With swift, slow; sweet, sour; adazzle, dim;
He fathers-forth whose beauty is past change:
          Praise him.

THE CAGED SKYLARK   ⫷⫷⫷   *Gerard Manley Hopkins*

As a dare-gale skylark scanted in a dull cage
   Man's mounting spirit in his bone-house, mean house, dwells—
   That bird beyond the remembering his free fells;
This in drudgery, day-labouring-out life's age.

Though aloft on turf or perch or poor low stage,
   Both sing sometímes the sweetest, sweetest spells,
   Yet both droop deadly sómetimes in their cells
Or wring their barriers in bursts of fear or rage.

Not that the sweet-fowl, song-fowl, needs no rest—
Why, hear him, hear him babble and drop down to his nest,
   But his own nest, wild nest, no prison.

Man's spirit will be flesh-bound when found at best,
But uncumbered: meadow-down is not distressed
   For a rainbow footing it nor he for his bónes rísen.

CROSSING THE BAR   ⫷⫷⫷   *Alfred Lord Tennyson*

   Sunset and evening star,
     And one clear call for me!
   And may there be no moaning of the bar,
     When I put out to sea,

   But such a tide as moving seems asleep,
     Too full for sound and foam,
   When that which drew from out the boundless deep
     Turns again home.

Twilight and evening bell,
    And after that the dark!
And may there be no sadness of farewell,
    When I embark;

For tho' from out our bourne of Time and Place
    The flood may bear me far,
I hope to see my Pilot face to face
    When I have crost the bar.

ANYONE LIVED IN A PRETTY HOW TOWN «« *E. E. Cummings*

anyone lived in a pretty how town
(with up so floating many bells down)
spring summer autumn winter
he sang his didn't he danced his did.

Women and men(both little and small)
cared for anyone not at all
they sowed their isn't they reaped their same
sun moon stars rain

children guessed(but only a few
and down they forgot as up they grew
autumn winter spring summer)
that noone loved him more by more

when by now and tree by leaf
she laughed his joy she cried his grief
bird by snow and stir by still
anyone's any was all to her

someones married their everyones
laughed their cryings and did their dance
(sleep wake hope and then)they
said their nevers they slept their dream

stars rain sun moon
(and only the snow can begin to explain
how children are apt to forget to remember
with up so floating many bells down)

one day anyone died i guess
(and noone stooped to kiss his face)
busy folk buried them side by side
little by little and was by was

all by all and deep by deep
and more by more they dream their sleep
noone and anyone earth by april
wish by spirit and if by yes.

Women and men(both dong and ding)
summer autumn winter spring
reaped their sowing and went their came
sun moon stars rain

A VALEDICTION FORBIDDING
MOURNING ⋘ *John Donne*

As virtuous men pass mildly away,
   And whisper to their souls to go,
Whilst some of their sad friends do say,
   "The breath goes now," and some say, "No,"

So let us melt, and make no noise,
　　No tear-floods, nor sigh-tempests move;
'Twere profanation of our joys
　　To tell the laity our love.

Moving of th' earth brings harms and fears,
　　Men reckon what it did, and meant;
But trepidation of the spheres,
　　Though greater far, is innocent.

Dull sublunary lovers' love
　　—Whose soul is sense—cannot admit
Absence, because it doth remove
　　Those things which elemented it.

But we by a love so much refined
　　That ourselves know not what it is,
Inter-assurèd of the mind,
　　Care less eyes, lips, and hands to miss.

Our two souls therefore, which are one,
　　Though I must go, endure not yet
A breach, but an expansion,
　　Like gold to airy thinness beat.

If they be two, they are two so
　　As stiff twin compasses are two;
Thy soul, the fixed foot, makes no show
　　To move, but doth, if th' other do.

And though it in the center sit,
　　Yet, when the other far doth roam,
It leans, and hearkens after it,
　　And grows erect, as that comes home.

Such wilt thou be to me, who must
    Like th' other foot, obliquely run;
Thy firmness makes my circle just,
    And makes me end, where I begun.

WHAT IF THIS PRESENT ⋘ *John Donne*

What if this present were the world's last night?
Mark in my heart, O Soul, where thou dost dwell,
The picture of Christ crucified, and tell
Whether that countenance can thee affright,
Tears in his eyes quench the amazing light,
Blood fills his frowns, which from his pierc'd head fell.
And can that tongue adjudge thee unto hell,
Which pray'd forgiveness for his foes' fierce spite?
No, no; but as in my idolatry
I said to all my profane mistresses,
Beauty, of pity, foulness only is
A sign of rigour: so I say to thee,
To wicked spirits are horrid shapes assign'd,
This beauteous form assures a piteous mind.

A REFUSAL TO MOURN THE DEATH, BY FIRE, OF A CHILD IN LONDON ⋘ *Dylan Thomas*

Never until the mankind making
Bird beast and flower
Fathering and all humbling darkness
Tells with silence the last light breaking
And the still hour
Is come of the sea tumbling in harness

And I must enter again the round
Zion of the water bead
And the synagogue of the ear of corn
Shall I let pray the shadow of a sound
Or sow my salt seed
In the least valley of sackcloth to mourn

The majesty and burning of the child's death.
I shall not murder
The mankind of her going with a grave truth
Nor blaspheme down the stations of the breath
With any further
Elegy of innocence and youth.

Deep with the first dead lies London's daughter,
Robed in the long friends,
The grains beyond age, the dark veins of her mother,
Secret by the unmourning water
Of the riding Thames.
After the first death, there is no other.

OH, NEVER SAY THAT I WAS FALSE OF HEART ⋘ *William Shakespeare*

Oh, never say that I was false of heart,
Though absence seemed my flame to qualify!
As easy might I from myself depart
As from my soul, which in thy breast doth lie.
That is my home of love. If I have ranged,
Like him that travels, I return again,

Just to the time, not with the time exchanged,
So that myself bring water for my stain.
Never believe, though in my nature reigned
All frailties that besiege all kinds of blood,
That it could so preposterously be stained,
To leave for nothing all thy sum of good;
  For nothing this wide universe I call,
  Save thou, my rose. In it thou art my all.

LINES: "WHEN THE LAMP IS SHATTERED" ⟪⟪← *Percy Bysshe Shelley*

I

When the lamp is shattered
The light in the dust lies dead—
  When the cloud is scattered
The rainbow's glory is shed.
  When the lute is broken,
Sweet tones are remembered not;
  When the lips have spoken,
Loved accents are soon forgot.

II

As music and splendour
Survive not the lamp and the lute,
  The heart's echoes render
No song when the spirit is mute:—
  No song but sad dirges,
Like the wind through a ruined cell,
  Or the mournful surges
That ring the dead seaman's knell.

III

When hearts have once mingled
Love first leaves the well-built nest;
  The weak one is singled
To endure what it once possessed.
  O Love! who bewailest
The frailty of all things here,
  Why choose you the frailest
For your cradle, your home, and your bier?

IV

  Its passions will rock thee
As the storms rock the ravens on high;
  Bright reason will mock thee,
Like the sun from a wintry sky.
  From thy nest every rafter
Will rot, and thine eagle home
  Leave thee naked to laughter,
When leaves fall and cold winds come.

ON FIRST LOOKING INTO CHAPMAN'S HOMER   *John Keats*

Much have I travelled in the realms of gold,
  And many goodly states and kingdoms seen;
  Round many western islands have I been
Which bards in fealty to Apollo hold.
Oft of one wide expanse had I been told
  That deep-browed Homer ruled as his demesne:
  Yet did I never breathe its pure serene
Till I heard Chapman speak out loud and bold:
Then felt I like some watcher of the skies
  When a new planet swims into his ken;

Or like stout Cortez when with eagle eyes
    He stared at the Pacific—and all his men
Looked at each other with a wild surmise—
    Silent, upon a peak in Darien.

THE SECOND COMING ⋘ *William Butler Yeats*

Turning and turning in the widening gyre
The falcon cannot hear the falconer;
Things fall apart; the centre cannot hold;
Mere anarchy is loosed upon the world,
The blood-dimmed tide is loosed, and everywhere
The ceremony of innocence is drowned;
The best lack all conviction, while the worst
Are full of passionate intensity.

Surely some revelation is at hand;
Surely the Second Coming is at hand.
The Second Coming! Hardly are those words out
When a vast image out of *Spiritus Mundi*
Troubles my sight: somewhere in sands of the desert
A shape with lion body and the head of a man,
A gaze blank and pitiless as the sun,
Is moving its slow thighs, while all about it
Reel shadows of the indignant desert birds.
The darkness drops again; but now I know
That twenty centuries of stony sleep
Were vexed to nightmare by a rocking cradle,
And what rough beast, its hour come round at last,
Slouches towards Bethlehem to be born?

THE GLASS OF WATER ⋘ *Wallace Stevens*

That the glass would melt in heat,
That the water would freeze in cold,
Shows that this object is merely a state,
One of many, between two poles. So,
In the metaphysical, there are these poles.

Here in the centre stands the glass. Light
Is the lion that comes down to drink. There
And in that state, the glass is a pool.
Ruddy are his eyes and ruddy are his claws
When light comes down to wet his frothy jaws

And in the water winding weeds move round.
And there and in another state—the refractions,
The *metaphysica*, the plastic parts of poems
Crash in the mind—But, fat Jocundus, worrying
About what stands here in the centre, not the glass,

But in the centre of our lives, this time, this day,
It is a state, this spring among the politicians
Playing cards. In a village of the indigenes,
One would have still to discover. Among the dogs and dung,
One would continue to contend with one's ideas.

4 ◀◀◀ define the context in
which the words are spoken

To grasp the meaning of the language of a poem is but the first step in understanding. One may know what all the words and sentences mean and yet not fully comprehend the poem, because a poem is not merely a series of sentences to be diagrammed. It is also an utterance that takes place in a certain context. Until you know who is speaking, where, when, and why, you will not fully grasp the significance of what is being said. The sentence "Pray you, undo this button" offers no problems of understanding at the verbal level. The individual words are simple and their grammatical relationship is straightforward. However, your interpretation of the full significance of the utterance will depend a great deal upon whether it is said to you by a friend having trouble with a starched collar, or whether it is spoken by an imagined old man at the moment when his mounting misfortunes are climaxed by the loss of his cherished daughter. The words when thus spoken by King Lear take on a terrible import. They are the cry of a man suffocating from the last wild beatings of a passionate heart.

It is useful to distinguish broadly between the two types of contexts suggested by our illustration: those in which the poetic utterance represents a direct communication of the author's ideas to his audience and those in which the utterance portrays a moment of imagined human experience. In the first case, the poem is best read as a brief expository or argumentative essay in verse. In the second case, the poem is best read as a brief form of drama or narrative, opening up windows upon the imagined affairs of particular men. Since poems asserting or arguing a proposition and those representing moments of drama require different analytical skills, let us consider these two basic types of utterances in more detail.

I

Let us first consider the poem that makes an *assertion*. The two parts of this type are the *subject* and what is said or *predicated* about it. A careful grammatical reading will allow you to distinguish between these two elements quite readily. It should be enough to remind you that an assertion may be about particular or general things. It may attempt to particularize the quality of a place, an event, an object, a person, or even the speaker himself (his preferences, moods, attitudes, motives, intentions, and so on). Or it may attempt to formulate a general truth. The techniques for clarifying and enlivening an assertion are numerous—for example, accumulation of supporting detail, illustration by analogy or example, analysis of parts, comparison and contrast, or formal definition. (These are more properly the business of Chapter 7 and will be taken up in some detail there.)

The following poem, by Robert Herrick, will serve as an example. (This poem and "To Lose One's Faith" will also be used as models in later discussions and have been reprinted on the fold-out sheet already mentioned.)

DELIGHT IN DISORDER

A sweet disorder in the dress
Kindles in clothes a wantonness:
A lawn about the shoulders thrown
Into a fine distraction,
An erring lace, which here and there
Enthralls the crimson stomacher,

A cuff neglectful, and thereby
Ribbands to flow confusedly,
A winning wave (deserving note)
In the tempestuous petticoat,
A careless shoe-string, in whose tie
I see a wild civility,
Do more bewitch me, than when art
Is too precise in every part.

The speaker in this poem is making a statement about himself, namely, that, because of its subtle invitation, he prefers "sweet disorder" to meticulous care in a woman's dress. He is not responding to any given situation such as a certain woman dressed in a certain way passing before him, and to whom he responds with a particular feeling of delight. He is not experiencing a moment of delight, but rather he is asserting that he is capable of such a feeling whenever he happens to see an attractive woman dressed in such and such a way. He simply suggests the basis of his feeling in the first two lines of the poem (a sweet disorder in the dress appears gay and erotically attractive), enumerates the various disorderly aspects of a woman's manner of dress which exemplify what he means (shawl, lace, stomacher, cuff, ribbands, petticoat, shoe-string) in the next ten lines, and concludes with a statement of preference in the last two lines. The technique that Herrick employs for elaborating his assertion is accumulation of details which explain what he means by "sweet" disorder as distinguished from other kinds of disarray.

II

The poem which not only places before the reader an assertion, but also urges him to accept it by means of supporting evidence—an *argument*—calls for one further step in understanding. It is not enough for you to grasp that such and such a thing is being predicated about such and such a subject. You must also understand which part of the poem presents the *conclusion* (the assertion) and which part presents the *reasons* (the *evidence* or *proof*), and you must perceive the force of the *logical implication* that allows the conclusion to be drawn from the evidence.

The following poem by Emily Dickinson will serve as a modest example of a poem setting forth an argument:

To Lose One's Faith

To lose one's faith surpasses
The loss of an estate,
Because estates can be
Replenished,—faith cannot.

Inherited with life,
Belief but once can be;
Annihilate a single clause,
And Being's beggary.

To understand the poem you need, first, to recognize that an assertion is being made in the first two lines to the effect that the loss of belief in God or some ideal is worse than the loss of worldly goods. Second, you must understand that lines three and four offer, not illustrations of the assertion, but evidence for it—namely, unlike an estate, faith, once lost, cannot be replenished. Finally, you need to realize that your mind is automatically supplying a generalization—that it is worse to lose what cannot be replaced than to lose what can be—in the light of which the logical relationship between the two sets of lines becomes intelligible. You should also note that the second stanza merely reasserts more vividly the evidence supplied in the last part of line four.

Some poems present far more complex arguments than we

have just encountered in Emily Dickinson's poem and call for more sophisticated skills in tracing out the logical implications of the *premises*. However, we have no inclination at this point to launch into a logical treatise. Suffice it to say that whatever principles you have learned in courses devoted to exposition and argument will not be out of place in considering the type of poem we have just been discussing.

III

The type of poem that portrays some particular human *experience* requires that you go beyond the analysis of subjects and predicates, conclusions and premises, to the dramatic circumstances in which the utterance is spoken. Statements and even arguments may appear here, but they arise as a *response* out of a specific *situation* in which the speaker or *protagonist* (whether representing some facet of the poet himself or someone imagined) is placed. *Situation* refers to the person's external circumstances at a certain moment in time—his fortune, his physical surroundings, his status and reputation, his health, what others do or say to him, and so on. Or it may refer simply to some question or problem, some internal or spiritual tension, that begins to press upon his awareness and call for consideration. Sometimes, furthermore, what looks like a situation may be only the apparent stimulus, serving merely to remind him of another and more truly causal situation. *Response* may refer either to an internal *reaction* of thinking or feeling, or to an external *action* of saying or doing, on the part of the protagonist.

In order fully to understand a poem that places a moment of human drama before you, you must grasp where the protagonist is (if there is a specific location involved), when (if this is relevant), who else is present (if anyone), and what the other person or persons have said or done (if anything), and so on—

in short, any and all aspects of his situation which are either stated or implied and which may help you interpret what he is involved in.

Next, you must realize what he is thinking, feeling, saying, or doing. In terms of what you have discovered about the meaning of the language in the poem, you may make inferences as to whether the protagonist is thinking (*perceiving*, or registering sense-impressions; *reflecting*, as in working out the relationships among things and ideas, seeking causes, making generalizations, interpreting the significance of things, becoming aware of facts and truths, making comparisons; *deliberating*, as in considering the factors involved in a course of action; or *meditating*, as in attempting to solve a problem, and so on); *feeling* (giving expression to some emotional reaction, as in hoping, fearing, wanting, delighting, deploring, and so on); or saying and doing something in relation to other people and his environment (acting externally or *persuading*, as in scolding, pleading, flattering, or commanding, or in putting some course of action into effect). The principles you use in making such interpretations are again not peculiar to poetry, but rather have to do with your general experience of life and your understanding of human behavior as being of certain kinds and as having certain causes. It is on this basis that inferences about situation and response may be made; and, furthermore, inferences may be made in a poem about the situation on the basis of the response, or about the response on the basis of the situation.

A human experience is thus a causal affair—this brings about that, or that is brought about by this. Your understanding of a poem will not be complete until you have clarified this *causal relationship*, for you cannot fully grasp a person's words unless you know why he says what he says and under what circumstances. But this is not all: also involved in this causal relationship is the very nature and temperament of the person involved, for different sorts of people will respond in different ways to a similar situation. Put a brave man under fire in a battle and he will stand fast; put a coward in the same position and he will run. Moreover the same person will react differently depending upon what he knows of his situation. Conceal from a man bent on revenge that his victim is the brother he has never known and he will pursue his course; inform him just who it is he aims to harm and he will hesitate or stop. Thus, in order to appreciate what is going on you must know not only the situation and the response but also the sort of person the protagonist is, his character, and the qualities and state of his mind and temperament. And these too are inferred from the details of the poem in the light of what you know about people and their motives.

There are, therefore, three aspects of a represented human experience which you must investigate before you can understand what is being put before you: what the reaction or action of the protagonist is (his response to a situation), what his moral character is, and what his state of mind is. It remains to define these last two a bit more fully. *Character* refers to a person's purposes and goals—what he seeks or avoids—and the strength of his will power in pursuing these ends. Such qualities may be good or bad, right or wrong, noble or base, strong or weak, and are revealed in the stands he takes, the decisions he makes, and the courses of behavior he abandons or follows. *Thought* refers to his conception of things, his habits of mind, his beliefs, the qualities of his temperament and sensibility, what he knows or doesn't know, his attitudes, and so on. Such attributes may be naïve or sophisticated, idealistic or cynical, ignorant or informed, cheerful or morose, and are revealed when he states general propositions or argues particular points. (It is possible to confuse character and thought, since they are both internal traits, but the difference between them and their logical independence of one another is quickly appreciated once it is recalled that, unfortunately, a person may *know* what's good but may nevertheless *seek* what's bad.)

Let us now return to "Desert Places" and ask what dramatic context gives rise to the utterance. Notice, first of all, that since the speaker's verbs are in the present tense, we can infer that he is in the scene as he speaks. It is true that in the second line is found "I looked into," but that is merely a sign, in terms of the poem as a whole, that he is situated just past the field after having looked into it as he went by (we can find no way of deciding whether he is walking or riding, but it is probable, since he seems to have gone past the field in only a few moments, that he is riding). It may be assumed, then, that he is riding on, after having passed the field. It is clear, furthermore, that he is alone. And what is his response to this situation? What is he doing? Not much of anything, apparently, for he is alone and is simply continuing on his way. There is, however, something going on inside him, for he is talking to himself—whether aloud or silently doesn't matter. And what is he saying? Just what we have been trying to interpret when studying the language of this poem! What it all adds up to is that the scene impresses upon him its desolation and sets in motion within him a deepening sense of emptiness, first in the farthest reaches of external nature and then, climactically, in his innermost being. This is what he is "doing": making mental connections, thinking, reflecting. The words in the poem arise out of the effect the scene has upon him and are a sign of the mental reaction which results, and they therefore must be interpreted as such.

Notice, further, that this reaction seems to unfold gradually and progressively as the speaker's experience continues throughout the poem. That is to say, his response is not merely a matter of a single moment, but develops through a succession of moments. An outline paraphrase of the poem as a whole will prove useful here:

First stanza: Speaker has just passed a field at nightfall and has noticed it filling up with snow.

Second stanza: This makes it seem to him as if the fields were being swallowed up by the surrounding woods, and that no signs of life remain to resist the oncoming snow and night. The animals have retreated to their lairs, and his own internal forces of spirit are dissipated.

Third stanza: His imagination begins to work beyond the immediate moment and he foresees that the field will appear yet more desolate as the snow piles higher.

Fourth stanza: His deepening awareness of the desolation of nature now leaps beyond the immediate scene to the vast emptiness of the solar system. At this moment the train of thought initiated by the snowy scene comes to a climax as he realizes that the most terrifying desolation is within himself.

So much, for the time being, about the speaker's situation and his response to it. We may now ask whether there is anything special about this man's attitudes and moral values which is needed to explain why his reflection takes the path it does. May any further inferences be made about the speaker's conception of things? He appears to be familiar with this part of the country, for there is nothing to indicate that all this is new to him, and he seems to be versed in country things, for he knows where the animals have gone. He seems, moveover, to be in a rather melancholy mood, and to be extremely perceptive about and sensitive to his surroundings. No simply keeping his eyes straight ahead on the road for him! It may be inferred that he knows something about modern science, and in particular about the new astronomy. It seems, finally, that he is concerned with the meaning of life and the things of the spirit.

What sort of character does he have? Can his moral traits

be determined? Would anyone have reacted similarly to the same circumstances? It's difficult to say, for the poem stops as he achieves his ultimate moment of insight and doesn't continue on to show him as taking some stand toward what he has discovered. Since inferences about a man's character depend upon the reader's knowledge of what he seeks or avoids, and since this poem does not show the reader any decisions being made, it must be concluded that no evidence as to the speaker's character is to be found.

The context of the language of "Desert Places," then, is that of a human experience in which a protagonist of a sensitive and philosophical cast of mind is shown responding to a desolate scene by relating that scene to the problem of his spiritual state and to the meaning of life.

poems for study and discussion ⫷⫷⫶

In assignments made from the following poems, after working out the meanings of the language as suggested in the preceding chapter, your problem is to identify the context of the poem in order to understand more fully its meanings. Decide, in the first place, whether the poem puts before you an experience, an argument, or an assertion. If it is an experience, decide next what kind of action or reaction the protagonist's response to his situation represents, what his thought is, and what his character is. (Since many poems representing an internal reaction involve no taking of stands, making of decisions, or putting courses of action into effect, it may be that character is frequently a neutral element.)

If it is an argument, separate the essential parts and identify which serves as the conclusion and which serve as the reasons.

If it is an assertion, decide if what is being put before you is an observation about a particular place, object, person, or event; or a general truth. Then, finally, define what is being said about this thing.

HEAVEN AND EARTH ⫷⫷⫶ *Coventry Patmore*

How long shall men deny the flower
   Because its roots are in the earth,
And crave with tears from God the dower
   They have, and have despised as dearth,
And scorn as low their human lot,
   With frantic pride, too blind to see
That standing on the head makes not
   Either for ease or dignity!

But fools shall feel like fools to find
(Too late informed) that angels' mirth
Is one in cause, and mode, and kind
With that which they profaned on earth.

A WOMAN'S LAST WORD ⫷ *Robert Browning*

Let's contend no more, Love,
Strive nor weep:
All be as before, Love—
Only sleep!

What so wild as words are?
I and thou
In debate, as birds are,
Hawk on bough!

See the creature stalking
While we speak!
Hush and hide the talking,
Cheek on cheek!

What so false as truth is,
False to thee?
Where the serpent's tooth is
Shun the tree—

Where the apple reddens
Never pry—
Lest we lose our Edens,
Eve and I.

Be a god and hold me
    With a charm!
Be a man and fold me
    With thine arm!

Teach me, only teach, Love!
    As I ought
I will speak thy speech, Love,
    Think thy thought—

Meet, if thou require it,
    Both demands,
Laying flesh and spirit
    In thy hands.

That shall be tomorrow,
    Not tonight;
I must bury sorrow
    Out of sight—

Must a little weep, Love
    (Foolish me!),
And so fall asleep, Love,
    Loved by thee.

ARS POETICA ⫷ *Archibald MacLeish*

A poem should be palpable and mute
As a globed fruit,

Dumb
As old medallions to the thumb,

Silent as the sleeve-worn stone
Of casement ledges where the moss has grown—

A poem should be wordless
As the flight of birds.

A poem should be motionless in time
As the moon climbs,

Leaving, as the moon releases
Twig by twig the night-entangled trees,

Leaving, as the moon behind the winter leaves,
Memory by memory the mind—

A poem should be motionless in time
As the moon climbs.

A poem should be equal to:
Not true

For all the history of grief
An empty doorway and a maple leaf.

For love
The leaning grasses and two lights above the sea—

A poem should not mean
But be.

A PORTRAIT ⋘ *Robert Louis Stevenson*

I am a kind of farthing dip,
Unfriendly to the nose and eyes;
A blue-behinded ape, I skip
Upon the trees of Paradise.

At mankind's feast, I take my place
In solemn, sanctimonious state,
And have the air of saying grace
While I defile the dinner plate.

I am 'the smiler with the knife',
The battener upon garbage, I—
Dear Heaven, with such a rancid life,
Were it not better far to die?

Yet still, about the human pale,
I love to scamper, love to race,
To swing by my irreverent tail
All over the most holy place;

And when at length, some golden day,
The unfailing sportsman, aiming at,
Shall bag, me—all the world shall say:
Thank God, and there's an end of that!

CARRION COMFORT ⋘ *Gerard Manley Hopkins*

Not, I'll not, carrion comfort, Despair, not feast on thee;
Not untwist—slack they may be—these last strands of man
In me ór, most weary, cry *I can no more.* I can;
Can something, hope, wish day come, not choose not to be.

But ah, but O thou terrible, why wouldst thou rude on me
Thy wring-world right foot rock? lay a lionlimb against me?
   scan
With darksome devouring eyes my bruisèd bones? and fan,
O in turns of tempest, me heaped there; me frantic to avoid
   thee and flee?

Why? That my chaff might fly; my grain lie, sheer and clear.
Nay in all that toil, that coil, since (seems) I kissed the rod,
Hand rather, my heart lo! lapped strength, stole joy, would
   laugh, chéer.
Cheer whom though? the hero whose heaven-handling flung
   me, fóot tród
Me? or me that fought him? O which one? is it each one? That
   night, that year
Of now done darkness I wretch lay wrestling with (my God!)
   my God.

A BIRTHDAY   *Christina Rossetti*

My heart is like a singing bird
   Whose nest is in a watered shoot;
My heart is like an apple-tree
   Whose boughs are bent with thick-set fruit;
My heart is like a rainbow shell
   That paddles in a halcyon sea;
My heart is gladder than all these
   Because my love is come to me.

Raise me a dais of silk and down;
   Hang it with vair and purple dyes;
Carve it in doves and pomegranates,
   And peacocks with a hundred eyes;

Work it in gold and silver grapes,
    In leaves, and silver fleurs-de-lys;
Because the birthday of my life
    Is come, my love is come to me.

THE ANIMALS   ⋘   *Edwin Muir*

They do not live in the world,
Are not in time and space.
From birth to death hurled
No word do they have, not one
To plant a foot upon,
Were never in any place.

For with names the world was called
Out of the empty air,
With names was built and walled,
Line and circle and square,
Mud and emerald;
Snatched from deceiving death
By the articulate breath.

But these have never trod
Twice the familiar track,
Never never turned back
Into the memoried day.
All is new and near
In the unchanging Here
Of the fifth great day of God,
That shall remain the same,
Never shall pass away.

On the sixth day we came.

A NIGHT IN NOVEMBER   ⋘   *Thomas Hardy*

I marked when the weather changed,
And the panes began to quake,
And the winds rose up and ranged,
That night, lying half-awake.

Dead leaves blew into my room,
And alighted upon my bed,
And a tree declared to the gloom
Its sorrow that they were shed.

One leaf of them touched my hand,
And I thought that it was you
There stood as you used to stand,
And saying at last you knew!

COME IN   ⋘   *Robert Frost*

As I came to the edge of the woods,
Thrush music—hark!
Now if it was dusk outside,
Inside it was dark.

Too dark in the woods for a bird
By sleight of wing
To better its perch for the night,
Though it still could sing.

The last of the light of the sun
That had died in the west

Still lived for one song more
In a thrush's breast.

Far in the pillared dark
Thrush music went—
Almost like a call to come in
To the dark and lament.

But no, I was out for stars:
I would not come in.
I meant not even if asked,
And I hadn't been.

WHAT IS OUR LIFE? ≪← *Sir Walter Ralegh*

What is our life? A play of passion,
Our mirth the music of division,
Our mothers' wombs the tiring-houses be,
Where we are dressed for this short comedy.
Heaven the judicious sharp spectator is,
That sits and marks still who doth act amiss.
Our graves that hide us from the searching sun
Are like drawn curtains when the play is done.
Thus march we, playing, to our latest rest,
Only we die in earnest, that's no jest.

TELL ALL THE TRUTH   ⋘   *Emily Dickinson*

Tell all the truth but tell it slant,
Success in circuit lies,
Too bright for our infirm delight
The truth's superb surprise;

As lightning to the children eased
With explanation kind,
The truth must dazzle gradually
Or every man be blind.

SPRING STRAINS   ⋘   *William Carlos Williams*

In a tissue-thin monotone of blue-grey buds
crowded erect with desire against the sky—
            tense blue-grey twigs
slenderly anchoring them down, drawing
them in—
            two blue-grey birds chasing
a third struggle in circles, angles,
swift convergings to a point that bursts
instantly!
            Vibrant bowing limbs
pulled downward, sucking in the sky
that bulges from behind, plastering itself
against them in packed rifts, rock blue
and dirty orange!
            But—
(Hold hard, rigid jointed trees!)
the blinding and red-edged sun-blur—

creeping energy, concentrated
counterforce—welds sky, buds, trees,
rivets them in one puckering hold!
Sticks through! Pulls the whole
counter-pulling mass upward, to the right,
locks even the opaque, not yet defined
ground in a terrific drag that is
loosening the very tap-roots!

On a tissue-thin monotone of blue-grey buds
two blue-grey birds, chasing a third,
at full cry! Now they are
flung outward and up—disappearing suddenly!

5 ⥸⥸⥸ ask what unifies the context

Once you have attained a secure understanding of the language of the poem and the context in which it occurs, you are ready to turn your attention to the problems of artistic organization. At this level of reading the aim is to grasp the organizing conception which synthesizes the elements of the poem (its shape, the manner of handling it, and its materials) in the service of an artistic purpose. There is no foolproof formula for seizing this organizing conception. It is not visible to the eye; it can be comprehended only by an act of the mind seeking a gestalt—a leap of the imagination from an awareness of the separate elements to an awareness of the principle unifying them into a system. However, we can offer you a useful hint: begin by asking what kind of unity or oneness the context itself has. In the case of the ax, for example, the shape of the cutting wedge is an important clue to its purpose.

It is one thing to recognize the difference between a moment of drama, an argument, and an exposition, and to locate and understand the various parts involved in each, but it is quite another thing to see how these parts are related to produce a unified context. To have a unified context means, first, that whatever is needed has been somehow included; second, that whatever has been included is somehow needed; and third, that these things are somehow connected according to a principle of relationship. Such notions are rather abstract; let us, therefore, show what they mean when applied to particular cases.

I

We shall consider the unity of a human experience first. The parts of this sort of context are, as we have shown, three: the protagonist's response to a situation (reaction or action), his thought, and his moral character. Now the principle of relationship which may connect these parts is *psychological causation*: a person thinks, feels, speaks, acts in a certain way *because* of something in his situation and *because* he has a certain cast of mind and, it may be, a certain kind of moral character. These three parts are, furthermore, capable of interacting with one another: not only may his reaction or action be influenced by thought and character, but also his thought may be influenced by his reaction or action and character, or his character may be changed by his reaction or action and thought. A person may seek revenge upon another because of some injury he feels the other has inflicted upon him and because he hasn't the proper moral values. His pursuit of this end may lead him to discover that his intended victim is his long-lost brother. And this in turn may change his moral values.

The first sense, then, in which the poet unifies his moment of human drama is that he takes one of its elements—action or reaction, state of mind, or character—as the central concern of the poem; that is, he develops thought and character for the sake of making a certain action or reaction intelligible, or he invents and develops a certain action or reaction and character for the sake of revealing and explaining a thought or feeling, or he makes use of an action or reaction and thought to reveal and explain a certain type of character.

The *principal part*, then, is basically what the poet wants to put before the reader, and this choice tells him some of the things he must do about the remaining parts. He is guided in these matters, therefore, not only in the sense that his choice of a principal part tells him that he needs to put forth or suggest certain subordinate parts, but also in the sense that it tells him what *sort* of subordinate parts he should consider appropriate to and consistent with the principal part. That is to say, if he wants to put before the reader a certain sort of reaction, then he must imagine that kind of protagonist—with certain specific qualities of thought and character—who would more likely than not (*probably*) or inevitably (*necessarily*) respond in that way to such and such a situation. If he wants, for instance, to show a man reflecting upon the briefness of man's stay upon earth, he must conceive of a protagonist possessing that sort of sensitivity and imagination which will be consistent with such thoughts; and similarly, if he wants to show a man deliberating upon a moral problem, he must imagine a protagonist having those qualities of character which will be appropriate to such an activity. Or, where the reaction or action is subordinate, if he wants to reveal to the reader a man of nobility of character or a man of sensitivity and imagination, he must invent a situation which would be likely to call forth those qualities in his protagonist.

The second sense in which the poet unifies his moment of human drama is that his choice of the principal part tells him what he must do with that part itself. Let us assume again, as an example, that he wants to put before the reader a certain sort of reaction, since that is most frequently the case with the poems in this book, and that he has conceived of those subordinate elements of thought and character which will suit his attempt to make that reaction intelligible. Now a protagonist's response to a situation may be of two sorts: it may be a single instant of reacting (*static*), or it may be a process of reacting covering a sequence of instants and involving some sort of development or change (*dynamic*); and a change may involve a single line of development (*simple dynamic*), or two or more

lines of development (*complex dynamic*). If a man responds to
the death of a loved one, for example, with an immediate and
single outburst of grief, then his reaction is static; if he responds first with a sense of numb shock and then gradually
becomes conscious of the sorrow of his loss, then his reaction is
dynamic and simple; and if he responds first with a lament,
but then reverses himself by thinking in a consolatory way
about the heavenly rewards which his lost loved one will receive
in the afterlife, then his reaction is dynamic and complex.

The unity of a static reaction demands that the poet put
forth or suggest only those aspects of the stimulating situation
and of the response which will contribute, as being more likely
than not or inevitable, to the presentation of that single reaction. This response may be merely one unalloyed instant of
thinking or feeling, or it may be an instant involving a mixture
of different impulses. But even in the latter case the mixture itself must be a single combination of things hinging upon one
sort of reaction or another. Secondly, if the poet takes a
single verbal request as his principal part, then his decision as
to what he wants his speaker to persuade his (the speaker's)
listener about will determine what would be a likely or inevitable
course of argumentation—as mediated by the appropriate
thought and character—for the sake of achieving that purpose.
If, finally, the poet decides to subordinate the reaction or action
to a revelation of the protagonist's cast of mind, or his moral
character, then he must attribute to his protagonist—either
explicitly or implicitly—only those traits of mentality and
temperament which will contribute to the presentation of the
sort of thought or character he wants to portray.

The unity of a dynamic reaction demands that the poet show
or imply a *beginning* point for the sequence of instants of his
poem, that he show or imply the consequent *middle* section of
this process, and that he show or imply a point at which this

process is brought to an *end*. And he must do this, as before, according to what would be appropriate to and consistent with the particular change—simple or complex—which he wants to present. This means that his beginning point, having nothing before it, must involve only those causal factors which could lead probably or necessarily to the middle; that his middle section, having something both before and after it, must involve only those causal factors which could probably or necessarily follow from the beginning and which could probably or necessarily lead to the end; and that his ending, having nothing after it, must probably or necessarily play out the consequences of all the causal factors which he has set in motion in the preceding beginning and middle. The end, that is, resolves the issue aroused at the beginning and developed through the middle.

When you are trying to decide which is the principal or unifying part of a poem, the first thing you should do is revolve all three alternative possibilities in your mind. If the reaction or action seems specific and particular, and if its elements and the factors of thought and character seem to be chosen primarily for the sake of portraying that reaction or action and making it complete and intelligible, then it is the main part; if, however, the reaction or action is not complete in itself, if all that the protagonist says does not arise out of the situation or bear upon the reaction or action itself, and if its elements seem to be chosen not primarily for the sake of its own consistency but rather for the sake of rendering the protagonist's thought or character and making that complete and intelligible, then it is one of these latter which is the main part.

How do all of these principles regarding unity and completeness apply to "Desert Places"? We have seen that the protagonist's reaction to his situation is one of thinking or reflecting (making mental connections in which his attention moves from the scene before him to the universe and then to his own spiritual state), that he has a sensitive and philosophical cast of mind, and that his moral character, apart from the fact that he is serious-minded, is not particularly in evidence. But which element of this brief drama is the principal part, principal in the sense that the poet's effort to make it complete and intelligible determines, to a large extent, what other elements of the poem he calls into being? As your reading skill improves, the answer to such a question about a poem will come more readily, perhaps even as you read it for the first time. Indeed, it is possible that the main element of "Desert Places" is already clear to you. However, for the sake of making our point, we shall suppose for the moment that it is not immediately apparent. What do you do then?

You ought first to consider, as we have suggested, what the alternative possibilities are and then try them out to see which one seems best to explain the parts of the poem and their relationship. In "Desert Places" there are, as we noted, three important elements of the drama: (1) the inward reaction of making mental connections which the scene calls forth in the speaker's consciousness, (2) his cast of mind, and (3) his character (insofar as this comes into play). Let us first ask if the setting is the main part. Is every other element of the poem subordinated to bring out some central quality of the snowy field—for example, its loneliness? The first two stanzas certainly support this possibility, for the choice of descriptive detail and the ominous personification of the surrounding woods indeed seem to be governed by the effort to vivify the quality of desolation. However, in the remaining stanzas the immediate scene is left far behind as the speaker's mind ranges to the stars and to the innermost reaches of the soul. Our first hypothesis, then, does not explain enough.

Is it possible that the main element is either the cast of mind or the character of the speaker, and that the scene, therefore, was chosen merely to bring out a characteristic response that would in turn reveal his central traits? Since cast of mind or character may each be one of the causes of a response, there is nothing perverse in taking that response as an index of thought or character. Indeed, the use of illustrative dramatic incidents is a favorite device in character portrayal. However, in the present case, there are two drawbacks to such an hypothesis. In the first place, it is difficult to determine just what mental or moral trait is being illustrated in the poem. Sensitivity to nature? But that scarcely explains why this particular natural setting should be chosen. Serious-mindedness? Again, this is too general a trait to explain the choice of scene and response. Spiritual despair? This hypothesis brings us nearer to the poem, but surely the sense of desolation is not a typical state of mind for the speaker. He is brought to a remembrance of his "own desert places" only by a special set of circumstances—circumstances that might induce melancholy reflections in any man of intelligence and sensibility. In the second place, any of the traits we have been able to think of fail to explain the immediate temporal sequence of the poem—its beginning, **middle, and end.**

We are left, then, with our final candidate, the inward activity of the speaker's ideas, which we have earlier characterized as an associative process whereby he moves from a contemplation of the wintry scene to an awareness of his "own desert places." We have only to state the hypothesis to sense that it is the right one, but let us consider in some detail just how the other elements of the drama are selected and organized in order to make this central process of reflecting complete and intelligible. In this view the setting is a subordinate part serving as a stimulus to make possible and credible the special train of associations started in the poem, and was thus chosen as a likely occasion in terms of which to stage the speaker's mental activity. Moreover, the thought and character of the speaker,

insofar as they are manifested in the poem, are also subordinate
to the train of association in the sense that they are kept consistent with that flow of thinking. For example, the quality of
sensibility revealed in the line "The woods around it have it—
it is theirs"—alert to overtones, exhibiting a hint of fancy, yet
sober in expression—is precisely the quality that helps make
plausible the mental leaps from one line of thought to another.
In other words, in order to present the particular line of mental activity he wanted to show, Frost had first to conceive of
his protagonist as having sufficient sensitivity and imagination
to respond to such a scene. He had to endow his speaker, furthermore, with a certain kind of imagination—one which concerns itself with spiritual problems, and with the relationship
between the meaning of life and the scientific knowledge of the
day—or else he could not have gotten his poem past the middle
of the third stanza. Now even though these things are not stated
in the poem, the poet must have had them somewhere in his
mind as he wrote, for unless he did we would have no other way
of accounting for the special quality and direction of the reflective activity manifested in the poem.

Character, as we have suggested, figures in the poem very
faintly if at all, for Frost has chosen to organize this experience
in terms of his protagonist having an insight. Since the revelation of what a person seeks or avoids and his willpower in doing
so requires by definition that he take some stand with regard to
his situation, that he come to some decision or attempt to accomplish something, character can be inferred only in poems
wherein the protagonist does more than merely think or feel.
In "Desert Places," for example, the speaker might conceivably
have decided, in an additional fifth stanza, to commit suicide as
a result of having such gloomy thoughts or to go home in order
to dispel those thoughts. If this were to be the case, however,
Frost would have had to go back over the poem and insert those

elements which would serve to prepare for such an outcome, and he would have had to re-think his conception of his protagonist in order to get those qualities of character required for the new ending settled in his mind. But as it is, no problem calling for a solution is suggested or stated in the poem as we now have it, and so it is complete as it is.

Not only does the effort to make complete and intelligible the speaker's advance from an awareness of an outer desolation to a consciousness of inner desolation help to determine the selection and organization of the other separable parts of the poem, but it also helps to determine the stages by which the advance itself is made. Everything that the protagonist says arises out of his situation and bears upon his reaction to it. As was indicated in our grammatical reading of the poem, it is quite easy to mark off the phases of this deepening awareness. The issue aroused at the outset is that of the speaker's relationship to the barrenness of the scene before him. From this it can be seen that, in beginning on a note of loneliness at the very outset ("But a few weeds and stubble showing last"), Frost was governed by the need of finding a suitable starting point to lead up to that sense of utter desolation which his protagonist would experience at the end. Now notice how the same principle governs the progress of the reaction so that the speaker's sense of loneliness and awareness of desolation become steadily and almost inevitably more and more intense: after the loneliness of the scene is established, the speaker relates his own inner state to it (thereby establishing a line of probability designed to lead, at the end, to the culminating shift from external to internal desolation); this leads naturally to his foreseeing that the physical scene will become even more desolate; this broadening awareness and his accompanying sense of the scene's expressionlessness naturally impel his mind out into the empty spaces between stars; and finally, as a result of all these things, he comes to an ultimate recognition of the bitterest desolation—his "own desert places." Since this recognition has a beginning point (first six lines) before which there is nothing and in which are placed the latent causes of what is to follow, since its middle (next six lines) follows naturally from this beginning and leads just as naturally to the end, and since the ending (last four lines) plays out the consequences of all the preceding causes— for there is nothing more desolate than an inner desolation— the speaker's reflection is complete. The issue of the speaker's relationship to the scene is thereby resolved. Even though it has to do with mental connections, its completeness is psychological rather than logical, however, for the progression toward a deeper and deeper sense of loneliness follows the probabilities and necessities of the speaker's mood and situation rather than the requirements of proof and demonstration. Once put in mind of a certain train of association, that is, he simply follows out its consequences until he reaches its end.

We must remind you, however, that what we have described just now is only the unity of the context. Although the shape of the experience is, as you have just seen, an important cause in determining the selection and handling of the several sub-ordinate elements of the poem, it is not the ultimate controlling factor. The wedge shape of the ax, you will recall, was not formed for the sake of its own internal symmetry, but for the sake of the purpose of the ax—cutting; so, too, the organizing process of reflecting that gives shape to Frost's poem is not for its own sake but for the sake of the poem's artistic purpose. How the artistic purpose of a poem is to be defined and how it is to be related to the other parts of the poem is the subject to be dealt with in the next chapter.

II

The unity of an argument differs from the unity of an experience in several important respects. An experience is unified if the response to a situation is a single process having a beginning, middle, and end, and if that process and its stages are made credible in the light of the character and state of mind of the protagonist; or if that response is assimilated into an effort to portray a certain character, or a man having a certain outlook. An argument is unified, on the other hand, if all the statements are brought to bear upon a single conclusion, and if these statements have a logical relationship to one another and to the conclusion. To discuss the nature of logical relationships in any detail would take us far afield. We shall trust that it is not difficult to discover the organization of an argument on a common-sense level. You simply begin by asking what the conclusion is and what evidence is brought forth to support it, as we suggested in the preceding chapter.

You recall that the conclusion of the argument in Emily Dickinson's poem—that the loss of faith is worse than any material loss—was supported by two reasons. One was explicit—the loss of faith, unlike a material loss, is irreparable—and one was implicit—it is worse to lose that which cannot be replaced. Whether these two reasons bear upon the single conclusion or not is easily resolved once you analyze their elements. Notice that each of these statements, including the conclusion itself, contains two basic parts, and that they repeat these parts in a certain way. The principle will become clearer when the argument as a whole is schematized as follows:

It is worse to lose (A) that which cannot be replaced (B).
The loss of faith, unlike a material loss (C), cannot be replaced (B).
It is worse to lose (A) one's faith than material possessions (C).

This scheme, as you may know, is called a *syllogism*, and it easily illustrates the way in which the conclusion derives from the two reasons or premises supporting it. There are only three elements in the entire argument, with the reasons repeating one each (B) and the conclusion repeating two $(A$ and $C)$. Nothing is said in the conclusion that is not already said in the premises. Thus are the reasons seen as bearing upon a single conclusion.

Not only must the conclusion derive from a combination of the two reasons supporting it, but it must also do so logically. This means, among other things, that A must include all things covered by B and that B must include all things covered by C. Unless this is so, the conclusion, which equates C and A by means of the prior equation of B with A and C with B, will not logically follow. You can see that if only some B's are included in A, then C might be equated with other B's that aren't, and that therefore C might equal A or it might not.

There are many other criteria for logical reasoning, but since they lie outside the scope of this book, we urge you to consult a good logic text if this aspect of poetic contexts particularly interests you. (You may find, as we indicated above, structures which resemble arguments in poems whose context is that of a human experience—in a meditation, for example, or a persuasion. We need only remind you that in such cases the poetic unity derives from the experience rather than the argument, and add that, although the argument may be logical, it need not be for the context to have unity.)

The other aspects of Miss Dickinson's poem—the use of inference, repetition, comparison—will be treated in Chapter 7. It is enough at this point for you to grasp the essential oneness of the context which it places before you.

III

The relationship which binds the parts of an assertion is neither experiential, involving psychological causes, nor argumentative, involving a syllogistic structure, but rather analytical, involving clarification. Such a context must put before the reader, by statement or suggestion, the thing which is being clarified (subject) and that which is being said about it (predicate), and connect these two parts in terms of that subject-predicate relationship. The description of a scene, for example, will put before the reader the various physical details of that scene (subject), will seize upon some aspect of that scene as its essential characteristic (predicate), and will unify this subject in terms of that predicate. Similarly, the exposition of a mood or preference or motive or attitude or intention will suggest or state that thing (subject) about which the speaker has a certain conception, will suggest or state that conception (predicate), and will unify this subject in terms of that predicate. A poem whose object is to explain to the reader the nature of some man's character or behavior will suggest or state those things (subject) in terms of which such a man's behavior will bring out his goals and willpower, will suggest or state those goals and that willpower (predicate), and will unify this subject in terms of that predicate. And the presentation of a general truth about something will suggest or state that which is being spoken of (subject), will suggest or state that which is asserted about it (predicate), and will unify this subject in terms of that predicate. Other aspects of such poems, such as offering reasons, exemplifying, or elaborating, will be treated in Chapter 7.

We have already shown that the parts of "Delight in Disorder" are, first, how a woman dresses (subject), and second, the speaker's preference for a sweet disorder in a woman's dress as opposed to a too precise neatness (predicate). Whatever he says in the poem, therefore, is unified in terms of that preference (predicate) with regard to how women dress (subject). When he includes these two parts and unifies them according to that principle, the context is complete. And that is all there is to an assertion: in this case, a single attitude expressed about a given thing.

To sum up, then, we have shown how the reaction of "Desert

Places," representing a reflective experience, has a beginning
and a middle and an end which are bound by necessity and probability in terms of psychological causation: the protagonist becomes aware of his own desert places not because there is any
logical connection between the scene before him, the empty
spaces between stars, and his spiritual state, but rather because
one puts him in mind of the other. We have shown, secondly,
how the structure of "To Lose One's Faith," representing an
argument, is unified in terms of logical relationships: it is more
deplorable to lose faith than something material not because
someone is in a situation but rather because faith is irreplaceable
and to lose that which is irreplaceable is deplorable. We have
shown, finally, how the announcement of "Delight in Disorder,"
representing an assertion, is unified in terms of subject-predicate
relationships: the speaker says he prefers a sweet disorder in
the dress not because he is in a situation or because there is any
logic to it but rather because he has a subject about which he
wants to predicate something.

poems for study and discussion ⋘⋘⋘

In assignments made from the following poems, after working out the meanings of the language and identifying its context as suggested in the two preceding chapters, your problem is to locate the principle binding the parts of that context into one whole and complete utterance.

If it is an experience, show the causal connections among action or reaction, thought, and character; decide which of these three is the principal part; and analyze the unity of this part itself.

If it is an argument, identify the premises (evidence), analyze their elements, and consider how they support the conclusion.

If it is an assertion, distinguish subject and predicate and show their connection.

THE POPLAR FIELD ⋘⋘⋘ *William Cowper*

The poplars are felled; farewell to the shade
And the whispering sound of the cool colonnade;
The winds play no longer and sing in the leaves,
Nor Ouse on his bosom their image receives.

Twelve years have elapsed since I first took a view
Of my favourite field, and the bank where they grew;
And now in the grass behold they are laid,
And the tree is my seat that once lent me a shade.

The blackbird has fled to another retreat
Where the hazels afford him a screen from the heat,

And the scene where his melody charmed me before
Resounds with his sweet-flowing ditty no more.

My fugitive years are all hasting away,
And I must ere long lie as lowly as they
With a turf on my breast, and a stone at my head,
Ere another such grove shall arise in its stead.

'Tis a sight to engage me, if anything can,
To muse on the perishing pleasures of man;
Though his life be a dream, his enjoyments, I see,
Have a being less durable even than he.

BINSEY POPLARS ⋘ *Gerard Manley Hopkins*

Felled 1879

My aspens dear, whose airy cages quelled,
Quelled or quenched in leaves the leaping sun,
All felled, felled, are all felled;
   Of a fresh and following folded rank
      Not spared, not one
      That dandled a sandalled
     Shadow that swam or sank
On meadow and river and wind-wandering weed-winding bank.

  O if we but knew what we do
      When we delve or hew—
   Hack and rack the growing green!
    Since country is so tender
  To touch, her being só slender,
  That, like this sleek and seeing ball
  But a prick will make no eye at all,

Where we, even where we mean
    To mend her we end her,
  When we hew or delve:
After-comers cannot guess the beauty been.
  Ten or twelve, only ten or twelve
    Strokes of havoc únselve
      The sweet especial scene,
  Rural scene, a rural scene,
  Sweet especial rural scene.

THE REVELATION   *Coventry Patmore*

An idle poet, here and there,
  Looks round him; but, for all the rest,
The world, unfathomably fair,
  Is duller than a witling's jest.
Love wakes men, once a lifetime each;
  They lift their heavy lids, and look;
And, lo, what one sweet page can teach,
  They read with joy, then shut the book.
And some give thanks, and some blaspheme,
  And most forget; but, either way,
That and the Child's unheeded dream
  Is all the light of all their day.

REVELATION   *Robert Frost*

We make ourselves a place apart
  Behind light words that tease and flout,
But oh, the agitated heart
  Till someone find us really out.

'Tis pity if the case require
   (Or so we say) that in the end
We speak the literal to inspire
   The understanding of a friend.

But so with all, from babes that play
   At hide-and-seek to God afar,
So all who hide too well away
   Must speak and tell us where they are.

HAP ⋘ *Thomas Hardy*

If but some vengeful god would call to me
From up the sky, and laugh: "Thou suffering thing,
Know that thy sorrow is my ecstasy,
That thy love's loss is my hate's profiting!"

Then would I bear it, clench myself, and die,
Steeled by the sense of ire unmerited;
Half-eased in that a Powerfuller than I
Had willed and meted me the tears I shed.

But not so. How arrives it joy lies slain,
And why unblooms the best hope ever sown?
—Crass Casualty obstructs the sun and rain,
And dicing Time for gladness casts a moan. . . .
These purblind Doomsters had as readily strown
Blisses about my pilgrimage as pain.

SONG: NO, NO, FAIR
HERETIC ⋘ *Sir John Suckling*

No, no, fair heretic, it needs must be
　　But an ill love in me,
　　And worse for thee.
For were it in my power
To love thee now this hour
　　More than I did the last,
I would then so fall,
　　I might not love at all.
Love that can flow, and can admit increase,
Admits as well an ebb, and may grow less.

True love is still the same; the torrid zones,
　　And those more frigid ones,
　　It must not know;
For love, grown cold or hot,
Is lust, or friendship, not
　　The thing we have;
For that's a flame would die,
　　Held down or up too high.
Then think I love more than I can express,
And would love more, could I but love thee less.

IF THOU MUST LOVE ME «
Elizabeth Barrett Browning

If thou must love me, let it be for naught
  Except for love's sake only. Do not say,
   'I love her for her smile—her look—her way
Of speaking gently,—for a trick of thought
That falls in well with mine, and certes brought
  A sense of pleasant ease on such a day'—
  For these things in themselves, Beloved, may
Be changed, or change for thee—and love, so wrought,
May be unwrought so. Neither love me for
  Thine own dear pity's wiping my cheeks dry:
A creature might forget to weep, who bore
  Thy comfort long, and lose thy love thereby!
But love me for love's sake, that evermore
  Thou mayst love on, through love's eternity.

THE EAGLE AND THE
MOLE «   *Elinor Wylie*

Avoid the reeking herd,
Shun the polluted flock,
Live like that stoic bird,
The eagle of the rock.

The huddled warmth of crowds
Begets and fosters hate;
He keeps, above the clouds,
His cliff inviolate.

When flocks are folded warm,
And herds to shelter run,
He sails above the storm,
He stares into the sun.

If in the eagle's track
Your sinews cannot leap,
Avoid the lathered pack,
Turn from the steaming sheep.

If you would keep your soul
From spotted sight or sound,
Live like the velvet mole;
Go burrow under ground.

And there hold intercourse
With roots of trees and stones,
With rivers at their source,
And disembodied bones.

IN MY CRAFT OR SULLEN ART ⋘ *Dylan Thomas*

In my craft or sullen art
Exercised in the still night
When only the moon rages
And the lovers lie abed
With all their griefs in their arms,
I labour by singing light
Not for ambition or bread
Or the strut and trade of charms

On the ivory stages
But for the common wages
Of their most secret heart.

Not for the proud man apart
From the raging moon I write
On these spindrift pages
Nor for the towering dead
With their nightingales and psalms
But for the lovers, their arms
Round the griefs of the ages,
Who pay no praise or wages
Nor heed my craft or art.

LOVELIEST OF TREES, THE CHERRY NOW   ≪←   *A. E. Housman*

Loveliest of trees, the cherry now
Is hung with bloom along the bough,
And stands about the woodland ride
Wearing white for Eastertide.

Now, of my threescore years and ten,
Twenty will not come again,
And take from seventy springs a score,
It only leaves me fifty more.

And since to look at things in bloom
Fifty springs are little room,
About the woodlands I will go
To see the cherry hung with snow.

VERSE IN PRAISE OF LORD HENRY HOWARD, EARL OF SURREY ⟪ *George Turberville*

What should I speak in praise of Surrey's skill
Unless I had a thousand tongues at will?
No one is able to depaint at full
The flowing fountain of his sacred skull,
Whose pen approved what wit he had in mew,
Where such a skill in making sonnets grew.
Each word in place with such a sleight is couched,
Each thing whereof he treats so firmly touched,
As Pallas seemed within his noble breast
To have sojourned and been a daily guest.
Our mother tongue by him hath got such light
As ruder speech thereby is banished quite.
Reprove him not for fancies that he wrought,
For fame thereby, and nothing else, he sought.
What though his verse with pleasant toys are fright?
Yet was his honor's life a lamp of light.
A mirror he, the simple sort to train,
That ever beat his brain for Britain's gain.
By him the nobles had their virtues blazed,
When spiteful death their honors' lives had razed;
Each that in life had well deserved aught,
By Surrey's means an endless fame hath caught.
To quite his boon and aye well-meaning mind,
Whereby he did his sequel seem to bind,
Though want of skill to silence me procures,
I write of him whose fame for aye endures;
A worthy wight, a noble for his race,
A learned lord that had an earl's place.

NANTUCKET ⋘   *William Carlos Williams*

    Flowers through the window
    lavender and yellow

    changed by white curtains—
    Smell of cleanliness—

    Sunshine of late afternoon—
    On the glass tray

    a glass pitcher, the tumbler
    turned down, by which

    a key is lying—And the
    immaculate white bed

6 ❦ define the poem's artistic purpose

We have now brought ourselves around full circle. In Chapter 2 we sought to show what we mean by the concept of a poem's organizing purpose and to explain the importance of that concept for our approach to poetry. We then endeavored in the subsequent chapters to show the successive steps by which one can track down, if it doesn't come at once, that organizing purpose in a poem. To this end we explored the problems involved in interpreting what the words mean (Chapter 3), what they reveal about the context of the poem (Chapter 4), and what kind of unity or shape the context has (Chapter 5). We are now ready to approach our main quarry—the effect the poem as a whole seems designed to have upon the reader.

Having come this far, you might well ask: just how does one make the final leap from the unity of the context to an understanding of the poem's organizing purpose? The context and the purpose are obviously not one and the same thing. To say a context is unified in such and such a way is to say nothing about the purpose or end-effect of a poem—except insofar as the presentation of any unified context will produce pleasure in the reader by setting up expectations as to what is coming next, holding them in suspense, and resolving them in such a way as to arouse both surprise and a sense of completion. But such general affective powers are merely the groundwork for the poem's particular impact upon the reader, which is more a matter of what specific impression these things are being used to support. Merely describing the wedge-shape of the ax-head, then, if we may once more unsheath our trusty analogy, and tracing the outlines of its graceful and efficient-looking structure, is not the same thing as defining the specific purpose of the ax—namely, to chop through wood.

How, then, does one proceed? The obvious answer would seem to be that you ought to examine your own feelings and attitudes as you read through the poem. How does the poem actually affect you? If you have understood the words and their context, and if you have a normal sensibility and an adequate range of experience, your response ought to be a good indication of the poet's purpose. There is much good sense in this reply. You cannot talk about the affective powers of a poem if you have not in reality experienced such powers, any more than you can discuss the harmonious effects of certain patterns of sound waves if you are tone-deaf. However, in order to verify whether your response seems to be the one designed by the poet or not, you have to move a step beyond subjective response. First, you must make as explicit a definition of the organizing purpose as you can; second, you must ask whether the poet's important artistic choices are indeed best accounted for as an effort to carry out that purpose.

In order to make explicit the organizing purpose of a poem you will find it helpful to have in mind some of the possible things that poets might set out to do. Broadly speaking, there are three. The poet may be primarily concerned with imparting knowledge in as vivid a way as possible. For example, he may wish to formulate in a striking manner some universal truth, or to convey the precise quality of some place, object, event, or person in the real world. Or again the poet may wish to do more than impart knowledge: he may wish to persuade his audience to accept a truth, to adopt an attitude, or to perform some action with respect to affairs in the real world. Thus he may praise something or someone, or satirize something or someone, or urge some mode of thought or conduct. Finally, the poet may give over instruction and persuasion in favor of setting forth an imagined human experience for its own sake, in the sense that he wants to elicit a completed emotional response on the part of the reader as that experience unfolds and resolves itself before the reader's inward eye.

When the context of a poem is an assertion of an idea (particular or general) or an argument supporting a conclusion, the problem of identifying the purpose is not difficult. To understand the language and the idea conveyed by the language and to recognize the relationship between the subject and predicate is to grasp the purpose of the assertion. Similarly, to understand the conclusion toward which all the evidence points in an argumentative poem is to perceive its purpose—colored, it may be, by a given emotional tone—whether it be to urge a truth, an attitude, or an action upon the audience. In the case of "Delight in Disorder," our example of an assertive poem, the reader perceives its purpose as soon as he grasps the poet's exposition of his special fondness for a wanton mode of feminine attire, and sees that it is to be taken in a light-hearted way. In the case of Miss Dickinson's "To Lose One's Faith," the reader's perception of the organizing purpose dawns at the very moment he recognizes that the poem is designed to show that the loss of faith is worse than the loss of something material, and realizes that this is to be taken seriously.

However, in the case of poems that have human experiences as their context, whether unified around action or reaction, thought, or character, the problem of defining the organizing purpose is a good deal more complex, for the poet may set forth such an experience for at least two different purposes. He may portray an experience, in the first place, for the sake of bringing out certain emotional qualities potentially contained in it and of shaping those qualities so as to have them strike the reader in the most complete and unified way; or, secondly, for the sake of some assertion or argument which that experience is shaped to exemplify or parallel or personify. In the first case, the capacity of an experience to arouse in the reader certain feelings is being developed for its own sake, while in the second case, this power is being used *rhetorically* for the sake of inculcating in the reader certain ideas or urging him to adopt certain attitudes or courses of action.

Let us consider the factors that must be taken into account in attempting to define the emotional capacities of any poem which has a human experience as its context, and then go on to consider the artistic role of those capacities. In broad terms, a reader's emotional response to an imagined person's experience depends upon three variables.

First, the reader's emotions will vary, according to whether the situation appears to be pleasant or painful for the protagonist, and according to whether such pleasure or pain appears likely to be permanent or only temporary.

Secondly, the reader's feelings will vary according to what sort of man the protagonist is—what estimate the reader is induced to form of his moral character and deserts and whether, in consequence, the reader tends to wish for him either good or bad fortune. The suffering of a good man produces different feelings in the reader than that of a bad man; a bad man enjoying himself makes the reader feel differently than does a good man in a similar state; and so on.

Third, the reader's feelings will be affected by the speaker's state of mind—whether the reader is made to judge what happens to him as being his responsibility or not, and if the former, whether he behaves in full knowledge of what he is doing or not. A man who does something terrible but without knowing the full extent of what he is doing will move the reader in a

DEFINE THE POEM'S ARTISTIC PURPOSE

different way than a man who commits the same crime in full knowledge. (It is relevant to recall here that even the law courts make such distinctions in meting out justice—the character of the accused and his motives are always important concerns.)

The affective powers of imagined human experiences fall into three classes when schematized in these terms. An experience which is to be taken as *serious* comprises characters who are conspicuously better or worse than ordinary or, if they are more like the ordinary, who can arouse in the reader strong sympathies; and the experiences in which they are involved result in marked pleasure or pain for them and have long-range consequences. A *comic* experience is one in which the characters are less than the ordinary in some way which is not painful for the reader to behold and whom the reader can favor, disfavor, or condescend to rather than feel hostile, friendly, or sympathetic to; and the events if painful are merely embarrassing, discomfiting, or ridiculous rather than permanent. Between these two extremes lies the merely *sympathetic* or *antipathetic* experience in which it is the experience itself which produces the effect rather than the morality of the characters: an action which is painful for the protagonist will produce pain in the reader, and one which is pleasurable will produce pleasure, and the personal traits of the protagonist are to a large extent indifferent as regards these effects.

If the poet, then, invents and fashions his human material with these principles in mind, the reader ought to find it useful to define his response to the poem in terms of these variables. Let us turn to "Desert Places" for an application. What does Frost seem to have tried to make out of the experience shown in this poem? In what way has he conceived of it? What impression does it seem he wanted it to make on the reader? Take the protagonist's situation and his response to it. The speaker is alone and feels the pressure of loneliness all around him. The scene before him is empty and without expression. As he senses these things, his mind turns toward the vast interstellar spaces which are correspondingly empty. He concludes that he has it in him so much nearer home to scare himself with his own desert places. It seems clear that, insofar as such a reflective process is an experience, it is a painful one, for the speaker sees a fearfully blank scene before him which he relates to his own fearfully blank places within. He is, in effect, in a state of chilled awareness, which elicits from the reader feelings of sympathy touched by pity.

And this is not merely the pain which any man might feel, but that which only a sensitive and imaginative one might feel. The reader's pity is thereby intensified, for he knows this speaker cares about such thoughts, that they are not random notions flitting in and out of his head, and that he has a responsible awareness of their implications.

This reflective process, then, is nothing light or temporary, but serious (for it involves matters of gravest import for man) and it has long range effects (for the awareness will become a part of his basic view of life). The protagonist's character is neither better nor worse than that of most men, and therefore his experience elicits the reader's sense of sympathy for one like himself. Further, we cannot blame this visitation of painful insights upon excessive morbidity on the part of the protagonist. They are insights that might come unbidden to a sensitive man aware of developments in modern science.

All in all, then, it may be said that Frost conceives of this experience as a serious and painful one and shapes it to make the reader feel a sympathetic shiver at the bleakness of the protagonist's reaction and a sense of pity evoked by his grim self-knowledge.

Once you have succeeded in defining your emotional response,

using the three variables we have discussed, the next consideration is whether that emotional response is enough to account for
the poet's artistic choices, or whether the emotional response
serves some further end. The way to do this is simple enough
in theory: ask whether the emotional capacities and powers of
the represented human experience are being developed for their
own sakes and as such appear to use up, as it were, all the
elements of the poem, or whether there seems to be something left
over after these powers and capacities have been accounted for.

In practice, however, the answer to this question often requires some hard thinking. Here are several rules of thumb to
bear in mind. The human experience portrayed in the poem is
probably serving some *rhetorical purpose* if (1) the poet has
not unified the experience in the sense we described in Chapter 5
(it is hard to imagine him representing an experience for the
sake of its emotional powers without his unifying it); (2) the
poet has added material which exceeds what is needed to portray
the experience itself effectively; and (3) the poet presents the
experience in such a way as to direct the reader's attention to
ideas beyond the immediate dramatic circumstances of the poem.

Before making up our mind about "Desert Places," let us
consider several clear-cut examples of poems which portray
human experiences but arouse emotional responses for rhetorical
purposes. Such poems are like assertions or arguments in their
ultimate ends and like dramatic poems in their means. But in
what ways may a human experience—or what resembles a
human experience—convey an assertion or argument? For one
thing, the experience may be presented as a particular example,
or *exemplum*, of a more general class. For example, in George
Orwell's *1984*, the protagonist, significantly called Winston C.
Smith, represents the average man in modern society. Or consider the following poem by E. E. Cummings:

NEXT TO OF COURSE GOD

"next to of course god america i
love you land of the pilgrims' and so forth oh
say can you see by the dawn's early my
country 'tis of centuries come and go
and are no more what of it we should worry
in every language even deafanddumb
thy sons acclaim your glorious name by gorry
by jingo by gee by gosh by gum
why talk of beauty what could be more beautiful than these heroic happy dead
who rushed like lions to the roaring slaughter
they did not stop to think they died instead
then shall the voice of liberty be mute?"

He spoke. And drank rapidly a glass of water

In this poem, we catch a glimpse of a patriotic orator in mid-speech. And it is a speech which is not complete in itself; indeed, it is merely a random string of patriotic clichés remarkably incoherent even for Fourth of July oratory. As for the speaker, we can only be repulsed by the mindless wagging of his tongue. What, then, can the purpose of such a poem be?

The first thirteen lines of this poem represent the quoted speech of our orator, while the last line is the quiet concluding observation of the narrator. Why cannot this be interpreted in terms of its emotional powers? Notice, in the first place, how exaggerated the orator's language is. This, coupled with his equally exaggerated praise of those who died in war, tends to make him appear ridiculous in the reader's eyes. But not merely as an object of laughter: the narrator's conclusion helps, by implication, to point up the absurd contrast between the orator's pompous speech and the trivial gesture of swallowing a drink in public, and this contrast helps to make the orator not merely absurd but especially absurd. Once the reader makes the connection between the realization that the orator is using the language everyone uses on public occasions to speak of the wartime dead and the awareness that the narrator is encouraging this view, he discovers that the orator is typifying hypocritical American public speakers and perceives something mindless and heartless in such a type. The purpose of this poem, then, is Cummings' attempt to bring the reader to this realization, and he has done so almost solely by allowing a typical character to speak in his own typically ridiculous fashion. The speaker and his oration, then, are represented as an example or instance of the kind of thing the poet wants the reader to despise.

A second way that an experience may convey an assertion or argument is by analogy or *parable*, that is, the experience may be presented, not as an example of a general class, but rather as a comparison to the actual subject of the assertion or argument. When Aesop set out to recommend courses of wisdom to his reader, he did not give direct advice. He told stories about animals and insects and relied upon the commonly accepted resemblances between the behavior of animals and insects and the behavior of human beings to permit the reader to construe the animal fable in human terms. Thus the tale of the industrious ant and the heedless grasshopper admonishes the reader by way of analogy to beware of the temptations of immediate pleasure. Parables are not necessarily limited to animals, however. In the following poem, Matthew Arnold presents a dramatic experience—the unfortunate accidental death of a lovely young bride in the midst of a festive occasion. But instead of developing the natural pathos of such an incident, Arnold turns our attention to the realm of ideas, for he sees in the circumstances of this accident a fitting analogy of his conception of the nature of poetry:

AUSTERITY OF POETRY

That son of Italy who tried to blow,
Ere Dante came, the trump of sacred song,
In his light youth amid a festal throng
Sate with his bride to see a public show.

Fair was the bride, and on her front did glow
Youth like a star; and what to youth belong—
Gay raiment, sparkling gauds, elation strong.
A prop gave way! crash fell a platform! lo,

'Mid struggling sufferers, hurt to death, she lay!
Shuddering, they drew her garments off—and found
A robe of sackcloth next the smooth, white skin.

Such, poets, is your bride, the Muse! young, gay,
Radiant, adorn'd outside; a hidden ground
Of thought and of austerity within.

A third way that a human experience may convey an assertion or argument is by *allegory*. Here, the human experience
stands in relation to the idea, not as example to class or as like
to like, but rather as a visible substitute for or embodiment of
the intangibles the poet wants to convey. Thus whatever is said
about the experience portrayed in the poem is understood to
apply to the subject which it embodies. For example, in *Pil-
grim's Progress*, John Bunyan presents a man making a journey to a desired land and on the way he has many adventures.
He passes through a treacherous slough, he descends into deep
valleys, he comes upon a village with a county fair in progress,
he is held prisoner in a castle, and so on. However, the events
of the journey are not told for their own sake but stand alle-
gorically for the spiritual progress of the good Christian as
he prepares his soul to meet his Maker. A modern example of
allegory occurs in the following poem by E. E. Cummings:

THREE WEALTHY SISTERS

three wealthy sisters swore they'd never part:
Soul was(i understand)
seduced by Life;whose brother married Heart,
now Mrs Death. Poor Mind

There is an action here—one sister is seduced by Life, one sister marries Death, and one sister is left a spinster—but it is clear that this action is not in itself a unified whole. In the first place, the people involved are not really people at all but rather *personified abstractions,* and thus the connections among them can hardly be those of human necessity or probability. In the second place, it is the narrator's commentary which concludes the piece ("Poor Mind"). As a result, in order to understand the meaning of the language of this poem, the reader is forced to decide what these "people" doing these things, in the light of the author's commentary, really "mean." The reader, that is to say, must translate the action into other terms: Soul, Heart, and Mind, were originally intended to be together, but they were separated by Life and Death, leaving Mind alone. What Cummings has to say here could be phrased somewhat as follows: man's faculties of spiritual insight, feeling, and understanding should be integrated into a harmonious whole, but they are not; the soul's powers are dissipated by the trivialities and distractions of physical life, the heart is distracted and enervated by fears of death, and the mind is divorced from all of them in sterile isolation. The implication is that the poet views this disintegration as something which is unfortunate. The action, then, is an allegory and exists for the sake of the idea.

All of these experiences are capable of arousing emotions in the reader—of disgust for the stupid orator, of pathos and wonder at the bride's death, and of pity for Mind the spinster—but they are obviously organized so that the reader's emotions are transformed from responses to experiences into attitudes toward ideas.

Now let us return to "Desert Places" and consider whether the action is developed to elicit a certain emotional response for its own sake, or whether that response is in the service of an assertion or argument. Is the experience complete? Our answer is yes. We are shown the circumstances that stimulate the reflective process of the protagonist; we are shown the successive phases of his deepening awareness of desolation; and, finally, we are shown the ultimate stage of the awareness. Does the poem present any elements in excess of this experience? Here our answer is no. The first line of the poem describes the scene which stimulates the protagonist's reaction and the last line presents the last phase of that reaction; nothing is extra in relation to this experience and its effective presentation.

The third question is the hardest to answer in practice: are there any clues that the experience refers to something beyond itself? It is possible for the reader to find an assertion or argument in any poem which presents a human experience, because there are bound to be motives and values involved which take shape as the experience takes shape and which are therefore likely to suggest to the reader a theme or insight into life. We could invent a doctrine for "Desert Places," for example, by making a parable of its context: as the speaker is brought to gaze upon his own inner emptiness, so too should modern science realize that its touch is death. Or an allegory: the speaker in his inner desolation is an embodiment of the Freudian death-wish. Or an exemplum: as the speaker is shown confronting external and internal emptiness, so too are all men in the modern world caught between meaninglessness without and meaninglessness within.

But the real question is not whether it is *possible* to find assertions or arguments in such a poem, but whether it is *necessary*

to do so in order to explain its organization. Notice that there
is no editorial comment as there is in Arnold's poem; there are
no allegorical labels as there are in Cummings' poem of the
three sisters; there is no incoherence, as in the jumbled oration
delivered by Cummings' politician.

Perhaps Frost's poem is still best read like these, you may
be thinking, although it is more subtle. Well, we can only return
to the poem itself and ask whether reading it in such a way
makes the poem and its organization any clearer. Our answer is
no. If it is a parable, it is surely not clear just what other
thing the speaker's experience resembles; we said modern science
only because we were looking for a plausible illustration of such
a possibility. If it is an allegory, it is similarly not clear either
that the speaker is an embodiment of something or what he is
an embodiment of. If he is in the grips of a death-wish—and
we don't even know that for sure (all we know for sure is that
he is becoming aware of an inner desolation of some sort)— it
is easier to see him as feeling it rather than as standing for it.

If it is an exemplum, and this is the most likely alternative,
then we are compelled to see him not as an individual but as
an instance of a type. He is caught, as indeed all modern men
are caught, between external and internal emptiness—or at least
as all modern men might be caught. But is he typical either in
his sensitivity to his surroundings, his awareness of deep issues,
or his ability to face himself honestly? Frankly, although it
would be flattering to most of us, we think not. Any literary
character must have certain traits which are shared by classes
of men, or else it would be difficult for the reader to comprehend his nature; and he must have certain traits which are his
own entirely, or else it would be difficult for the reader to find
any interest in his portrayal. The point is that in a true exemplum the typical traits outweigh the individual ones. In a
poem presenting an experience for its own sake the individual

traits will outweigh the typical ones. Frost's poem is, we believe, of the latter kind.

So far we have offered you practical steps for making explicit the organizing purpose of the poem solely on the basis of the way the poet has conceived and shaped his context. But there is another important aspect of a poem which contributes to its affective power and which consequently provides clues for and confirmations of the reader's hypothesis regarding its organizing purpose, namely, the way in which this context is put before the reader. We shall take up this aspect in the next two chapters.

poems for study and discussion ⫷⫷

In assignments made from the following poems, after working out the meanings of the language, identifying its context, and analyzing unity of its context as suggested in the three preceding chapters, your problem is to define the organizing purpose which seems to account for the special way in which that context is conceived and shaped.

If it is an assertion, define the relationship between the subject and predicate and specify the emotional light in which it is to be taken.

If it is an argument, define the relationship between the premises and conclusion and specify the manner in which it is to be viewed.

If it is an experience, determine whether the emotional effect seems to be serious, comic, sympathetic or antipathetic, in terms of the pleasures and pains of the protagonist's situation and response, his moral deserts, and the extent of his responsibility. If the experience seems not to be the main purpose, consider the possibility that it may be designed to serve a further purpose, whether as a parable, exemplum, or allegory.

JOURNEY OF THE MAGI ⫷⫷ *T. S. Eliot*

'A cold coming we had of it,
Just the worst time of the year
For a journey, and such a long journey:
The ways deep and the weather sharp,
The very dead of winter.'

And the camels galled, sore-footed, refractory,
Lying down in the melting snow.
There were times we regretted
The summer palaces on slopes, the terraces,
And the silken girls bringing sherbet.
Then the camel men cursing and grumbling
And running away, and wanting their liquor and women,
And the night-fires going out, and the lack of shelters,
And the cities hostile and the towns unfriendly
And the villages dirty and charging high prices:
A hard time we had of it.
At the end we preferred to travel all night,
Sleeping in snatches,
With the voices singing in our ears, saying
That this was all folly.
Then at dawn we came down to a temperate valley,
Wet, below the snow line, smelling of vegetation;
With a running stream and a water-mill beating the darkness,
And three trees on the low sky,
And an old white horse galloped away in the meadow.

Then we came to a tavern with vine-leaves over the lintel,
Six hands at an open door dicing for pieces of silver,
And feet kicking the empty wine-skins.
But there was no information, and so we continued
And arrived at evening, not a moment too soon
Finding the place; it was (you may say) satisfactory.

All this was a long time ago, I remember,
And I would do it again, but set down
This set down
This: were we led all that way for

Birth or Death? There was a Birth, certainly,
We had evidence and no doubt. I had seen birth and death,
But had thought they were different; this Birth was
Hard and bitter agony for us, like Death, our death.
We returned to our places, these Kingdoms,
But no longer at ease here, in the old dispensation,
With an alien people clutching their gods.
I should be glad of another death.

FABLE ⋘ *Ralph Waldo Emerson*

The mountain and the squirrel
Had a quarrel;
And the former called the latter "Little Prig."
Bun replied,
"You are doubtless very big;
But all sorts of things and weather
Must be taken in together
To make up a year
And a sphere.

And I think it's no disgrace
To occupy my place.
If I'm not so large as you,
You are not so small as I,
And not half so spry.
I'll not deny you make
A very pretty squirrel track;
Talents differ: all is well and wisely put;
If I cannot carry forests on my back,
Neither can you crack a nut."

LUCIFER IN STARLIGHT   *George Meredith*

On a starred night Prince Lucifer uprose.
Tired of his dark dominion swung the fiend
Above the rolling ball in cloud part screened,
Where sinners hugged their specter of repose.
Poor prey to his hot fit of pride were those.
And now upon his western wing he leaned,
Now his huge bulk o'er Afric's sands careened,
Now the black planet shadowed Arctic snows.
Soaring through wider zones that pricked his scars
With memory of the old revolt from Awe,
He reached a middle height, and at the stars,
Which are the brain of heaven, he looked, and sank.
Around the ancient track marched, rank on rank,
The army of unalterable law.

FOR A DEAD LADY   *Edwin Arlington Robinson*

No more with overflowing light
Shall fill the eyes that now are faded,
Nor shall another's fringe with night
Their woman-hidden world as they did.
No more shall quiver down the days
The flowing wonder of her ways,
Whereof no language may requite
The shifting and the many-shaded.

The grace, divine, definitive,
Clings only as a faint forestalling;
The laugh that love could not forgive

Is hushed, and answers to no calling;
The forehead and the little ears
Have gone where Saturn keeps the years;
The breast where roses could not live
Has done with rising and with falling.

The beauty, shattered by the laws
That have creation in their keeping,
No longer trembles at applause,
Or over children that are sleeping;
And we who delve in beauty's lore
Know all that we have known before
Of what inexorable cause
Makes Time so vicious in his reaping.

HERE LIES A LADY   ≪≪≪   *John Crowe Ransom*

Here lies a lady of beauty and high degree.
Of chills and fever she died, of fever and chills,
The delight of her husband, her aunts, an infant of three,
And of medicos marveling sweetly on her ills.

For either she burned, and her confident eyes would blaze,
And her fingers fly in a manner to puzzle their heads—
What was she making? Why, nothing; she sat in a maze
Of old scraps of laces, snipped into curious shreds—

Or this would pass, and the light of her fire decline
Till she lay discouraged and cold like a thin stalk white and
    blown,

And would not open her eyes, to kisses, to wine;
The sixth of these states was her last; the cold settled down.

Sweet ladies, long may ye bloom, and toughly I hope ye may
    thole,
But was she not lucky? In flowers and lace and mourning,
In love and great honor we bade God rest her soul
After six little spaces of chill, and six of burning.

GOD'S GRANDEUR ⫷ *Gerard Manley Hopkins*

The world is charged with the grandeur of God.
It will flame out, like shining from shook foil;
It gathers to a greatness, like the ooze of oil
Crushed. Why do men then now not reck his rod?
Generations have trod, have trod, have trod;
And all is seared with trade; bleared, smeared with toil;
And wears man's smudge and shares man's smell: the soil
Is bare now, nor can foot feel, being shod.

And for all this, nature is never spent;
There lives the dearest freshness deep down things;
And though the last lights off the black West went
Oh, morning, at the brown brink eastward, springs—
Because the Holy Ghost over the bent
World broods with warm breast and with ah! bright wings.

THE RED WHEELBARROW ⋘
William Carlos Williams

so much depends
upon

a red wheel
barrow

glazed with rain
water

beside the white
chickens

A MAN SAW A BALL OF GOLD IN THE SKY ⋘ Stephen Crane

A man saw a ball of gold in the sky;
He climbed for it,
And eventually he achieved it—
It was clay.

Now this is the strange part:
When the man went to the earth
And looked again,
Lo, there was the ball of gold.
Now this is the strange part:
It was a ball of gold.
Ay, by the heavens, it was a ball of gold.

THE TROOPER ⋘ *Alexander Brome*

Come, come, let us drink,
'Tis in vain to think
   Like fools on grief or sadness;
Let our money fly
And our sorrows die,
   All our worldly care is madness;
But sack and good cheer
Will in spite of our fear
   Inspire our souls with gladness.

Let the greedy clowns
That do live like hounds,
   That know neither bound nor measure,
Lament each loss,
For their wealth is their cross,
   Whose delight is in their treasure;
But we that have none,
Will use theirs as our own,
   And spend it at our pleasure.

Troll about the bowl,
The delight of my soul,
   And to my hand commend it.
A fig for a chink,
'Twas made to buy drink,
   Before that we go we'll end it;
When we've spent our store,
The land will yield us more,
   And jovially we will spend it.

ODE ON THE DEATH OF A FAVOURITE CAT, DROWNED IN A TUB OF GOLD FISHES ⋘ *Thomas Gray*

'Twas on a lofty vase's side,
Where China's gayest art had dy'd
  The azure flowers, that blow;
Demurest of the tabby kind,
The pensive Selima reclin'd,
  Gazed on the lake below.

Her conscious tail her joy declar'd;
The fair round face, the snowy beard,
  The velvet of her paws,
Her coat, that with the tortoise vies,
Her ears of jet, and emerald eyes,
  She saw; and purr'd applause.

Still had she gaz'd; but 'midst the tide
Two angel forms were seen to glide,
  The Genii of the stream:
Their scaly armour's Tyrian hue
Thro' richest purple to the view
  Betray'd a golden gleam.

The hapless Nymph with wonder saw:
A whisker first and then a claw,
  With many an ardent wish,
She stretch'd in vain to reach the prize.
What female heart can gold despise?
  What Cat's averse to fish?

Presumptuous Maid! with looks intent
Again she stretch'd, again she bent,
　　Nor knew the gulf between.
(Malignant Fate sat by, and smil'd)
The slipp'ry verge her feet beguil'd,
　　She tumbled headlong in.

Eight times emerging from the flood
She mew'd to ev'ry watry God,
　　Some speedy aid to send.
No Dolphin came, no Nereid stirr'd:
Nor cruel *Tom* nor *Susan* heard.
　　A Fav'rite has no friend!

From hence, ye Beauties, undeceiv'd,
Know, one false step is ne'er retriev'd,
　　And be with caution bold.
Not all that tempts your wand'ring eyes
And heedless hearts, is lawful prize;
　　Nor all, that glisters, gold.

THE SOUL SELECTS HER OWN SOCIETY ≪ *Emily Dickinson*

The soul selects her own society,
Then shuts the door;
On her divine majority
Obtrude no more.

Unmoved, she notes the chariot's pausing
At her low gate;
Unmoved, an emperor is kneeling
Upon her mat.

I've known her from an ample nation
Choose one;
Then close the valves of her attention
Like stone.

WOMEN ⋘ *Louise Bogan*

Women have no wilderness in them,
They are provident instead,
Content in the tight hot cell of their hearts
To eat dusty bread.

They do not see cattle cropping red winter grass,
They do not hear
Snow water going down under culverts
Shallow and clear.

They wait, when they should turn to journeys,
They stiffen, when they should bend.
They use against themselves that benevolence
To which no man is friend.

They cannot think of so many crops to a field
Or of clean wood cleft by an ax.
Their love is an eager meaninglessness
Too tense, or too lax.

They hear in every whisper that speaks to them
A shout and a cry.
As like as not, when they take life over their door-sills
They should let it go by.

THE BLOODY SIRE   «« *Robinson Jeffers*

It is not bad. Let them play.
Let the guns bark and the bombing-plane
Speak his prodigious blasphemies.
It is not bad, it is high time,
Stark violence is still the sire of all the world's values.

What but the wolf's tooth whittled so fine
The fleet limbs of the antelope?
What but fear winged the birds, and hunger
Jeweled with such eyes the great goshawk's head?
Violence has been the sire of all the world's values.

Who would remember Helen's face
Lacking the terrible halo of spears?
Who formed Christ but Herod and Caesar,
The cruel and bloody victories of Caesar?
Violence, the bloody sire of all the world's values.

Never weep, let them play,
Old violence is not too old to beget new values.

7 ⋘ ask how the artistic purpose
is served by technique

A given context conceived in a certain way has certain potential affective powers over the reader's feelings and opinions and actions. But it is the way in which this context is put before the reader which serves to embody and make vivid these powers. And under this latter question there are two factors to take into account: first, *technique*, or the manner in which the context is unfolded, and second, *style*, or the language which is used for doing so. We shall take up the first topic in this chapter, reserving the second for the following chapter.

What do we mean by the manner in which the context is unfolded? Imagine the decisions which must be faced by the director of a motion picture after his writers have delivered him a script: he has a story to film, but now he must decide *how* it is to be filmed in order to project that story most effectively before the movie-goer. He must decide, for example, whether to show the story directly to the audience through the camera's eye or to interpose between the story and the audience one of the characters as a narrator. He must decide, whether during shooting or later in the cutting room, what belongs in the completed version and what should be left out. He must decide, during the progress of any given scene, whether to bring the camera in for a closeup or to bring it back for a long shot; whether to film the scene step by step as it occurs or to speed it up and hurry through it; how to make his transitions from one scene to another; and so on. He must decide whether to start at the beginning of the story and proceed chronologically on to the end or to start somewhere after the beginning and

bring in earlier material through flashbacks. These and many
more are problems of technique.

The poet must likewise make a range of choices in "projec-
ting" his poem to make it both intelligible and vivid, and to do
so with the greatest economy of means consistent with his purpose. One problem he must face is to determine the *point of
view:* he must decide who shall utter his poem and whether this
shall be done in the present or the past. There are three possibilities as to the choice of speaker: the protagonist himself,
some other person within the frame of the experience, or the
author himself. The protagonist may speak in his own voice as
he undergoes the experience, and this is called the *present* or
dramatic point of view. If there is an action involving the behavior of others, and if they speak in their own voices in the
present, then this too is the dramatic point of view. This is
the normal manner in which plays are put before the reader or
audience, but poems and stories and novels may use it as well.
The protagonist may speak in his own voice but from a point
in time after the experience has occurred; this is called the
point of view of the *protagonist-narrator.* Another person
within the frame of the experience may recount the experience
after it happened; this is called the point of view of the *witness-
narrator.* Or the author may tell it after it happened; this is
called the point of view of the *omniscient-narrator*—"omniscient" because, since the author is not a part of the experience,
he can peer into the minds of his people and shift time and place
at will. Combinations and variations of these points of view
are possible, but these are the main kinds in terms of which
variations may be defined.

Another problem the poet must face is that of *selection.* He
must decide what goes in and what should be left out; and if
left out, whether it should be left to inference, or be left to
occur "offstage" and be narrated somehow, or forgotten alto-

gether. What he has to decide about may be seen in terms of a threefold distinction: there are those parts, first, which are essential to the very unity of his context itself—the causal line of an experience, the syllogistic parts of an argument, and the subject and predicate of an exposition; these are the *primary structural parts*. There are, second, parts which are structural but which serve merely to bring the primary structural parts into view; these are called *subordinate* or *secondary structural parts*. There are, third, parts which are not a part of the structure but which serve merely to clarify and vivify those parts which are structural; these are called *representational parts*. Thus an author, in the service of a given effect, may include in his poem less than his context, or more, or just as much.

Another problem the poet faces is that of *scale*. Having decided what to include, he must decide what should be given lengthy and detailed treatment, what should be skimped and hurried over, and what should be handled somewhere in between. It all has reference to what he wants to clarify and emphasize, and one way of clarifying and emphasizing is to *expand* and elaborate. Economy and de-emphasis, on the other hand, are encouraged by *condensing* and contracting. Or, in certain instances, emphasis may be produced by judicious brevity.

The last problem of manner the poet faces is that of *order*. He must decide what principle of sequence he will use in arranging the elements which are included. If he is representing an experience, he may choose to unfold his story *chronologically* or he may decide to begin somewhere after the beginning and work back and forth *achronologically*. If he is presenting an argument, he may proceed logically from major premise to minor premise to conclusion, or he may rework this order in some other way. If he is presenting an exposition, he may proceed from subject to predicate or vice versa, or he may use some other pattern—such as statement and illustration, comparison and contrast, some spatial order, some plan of repetition and variation, an order of ascending or descending importance, or a plan of introduction and body and conclusion, and so on. And these principles of sequence may of course appear in combination and be used with any of the three basic contexts.

It's all a question of unfolding, then, in relation to the effect the poet wants his poem to have upon the reader: unfolding of what (selection), in what light (point of view), to what extent (scale), and in what sequence (order). We turn now to exemplify these principles.

I

Yet another visit to "Desert Places." The experience is shown from the dramatic point of view, for the protagonist is speaking as he undergoes the experience in the present. This choice is dictated by several considerations. If the poet's aim is to evoke the reader's pity and sympathy for a single character undergoing a series of more or less painful reflections, then it will serve this purpose best to show that experience as it actually happens, for direct presentation creates the most vivid image. This means, moreover, that he can show the reader his speaker's reflections in the very process of unfolding, and thereby have the reader follow them point by point. Thus, when the end is reached, the reader has been prepared by a gradual and present process of revelation, and is therefore in the proper mood to understand and appreciate the full force of the final insight.

Regarding selection, notice that Frost decided to include the whole experience, as it unfolds, in the poem. Each stanza helps to carry forward the speaker's deepening awareness of desolation: he notices the field disappearing under snow, he thinks of the absence of life, he imagines how the scene will grow even more barren, he becomes aware of the desolation of the stellar spaces, and finally he plumbs the depths of his own emptiness. There is nothing more here than the whole reaction, and there is nothing less. Thus are the reader's sympathies and sense of pity deepened by putting before him clearly and vividly the experience in all of its stages. If Frost had left the beginning to inference, the reader would probably not be prepared to appreciate the meaning and weight of the culminating insight; if he had merely suggested the end, the reader would probably be at a loss in guessing at a mystery which is mysterious enough when actually presented; or if he had skimped in his presentation of the developing middle stages of the reflection, the reader would probably not be disposed to believe in the leap the speaker's mind takes between the beginning and end.

As for the scaling of these stages of awareness, you will notice that the first three are each allotted a stanza for development, while the last two stages are compressed within the span of a single stanza. This change in scale not only reflects the accelerating pace of the speaker's flow of ideas as his imagination takes hold, but it also coincides effectively with his sudden shock of recognition that his own spiritual state is the most frightening aspect of the experience. Thus is the reader prepared in yet another way to receive the full force of the culminating conclusion.

The poet's decisions regarding order or sequence are to a certain extent related to his decision as to point of view, because the framework he chooses for his story establishes certain limits on how he can arrange its elements. Since the experience is told from the protagonist's present point of view, and since a man who speaks his ideas as he experiences them can only follow their actual chronological order, Frost had to begin at the beginning, proceed along through the middle, and then reach the end of the experience at the end of the poem.

Such, then, are several of the choices regarding techniques of representation which Frost confronted and resolved in accordance with his artistic aim.

II

What about Emily Dickinson's poem? Since there is no one responding to a situation, the point of view can be neither dramatic nor that of a protagonist- or witness-narrator, but is rather that of the omniscient author speaking in the present. Since she is arguing a conclusion about the way things are, it seems proper for her to speak in the present: to lose one's faith surpasses the loss of something material, now, in the past, and in the future—that is to say, this is true in general. Furthermore, it behooves her, if she is to be persuasive, to speak in the character of one whom her supposed audience can trust, and this means in turn that she must entertain some sort of conception as to the nature of that audience. These are slight matters in such a small poem and are more easily discussed in reference to argumentative poems of somewhat greater length and scope, but even here it may be inferred that the omniscient author speaks in the character of a serious, thoughtful, and even devout person, and that she conceives of her audience as being somewhat less spiritually-minded.

How such an inference may be made will become clear in a moment. Regarding the selection of parts, several things should be noticed. First, persuasiveness requires that she choose reasons which will appeal to her audience: if she is going to argue that the loss of faith is worse than any material loss, she must find convincing reasons. She chose to argue on the ground that faith cannot be replaced while material things can, and if her audience is a bit more inclined toward the material than the spiritual, this seems quite apt. Second is the fact the she left the other reason—that it is worse to lose that which cannot be replaced—to inference, for it is perfectly obvious and need not take up space in the poem.

Third, and most important, is the instance of material loss she uses to place her argument in the proper light—and this is a representational part. This choice perhaps tells us something about Miss Dickinson's conception of her audience, for an estate is one of the most important of material goods and it is clear that she assumed her audience would most easily understand the gravity of such a loss. If most people regard the loss of an inheritance as being as bad a thing as can be imagined, and if it can be shown that losing faith is worse than losing an estate, then it will follow that the loss of faith is bad indeed. Hence the poet points out that, while both can be lost, only faith is irreplaceable. Thus the argument is placed in its proper light and its affective force made vivid.

As far as scaling is concerned, you should notice that the second stanza amplified the statement that faith cannot be replaced. As this is, after all, her most telling reason, it seems to call for emphasis. And with regard to the order of an argument, the reasons may either precede the conclusion or they may follow it. Here, you may have noticed that the reasons are placed after the conclusion. With the conclusion in mind, the reader can more readily grasp the relevance of the reasons.

III

"Delight in Disorder" is spoken by the protagonist in the present. This seems effective, since the speaker wants to inform us how he feels about the way women dress, and the present tense here functions in the same way as in "To Lose One's Faith," for Herrick too speaks of what is customarily true.

His selection of elements is interesting. The basic unity of the context—a certain attitude—is complete in the first two and the last two lines:

A sweet disorder in the dress
Kindles in clothes a wantonness . . .
[Which doth] more bewitch me, than when art
Is too precise in every part.

The subject is stated in the first two lines and the predicate in the last two; this constitutes the body of the assertion. But as such it is not very interesting, and it is the function of the middle ten lines to provide that interest. And that they do by supplying examples of that sort of sweet disorder which bewitches the speaker: there are five of these examples, and they are representational parts. Sometimes, as is perhaps the case in this poem, the interest of such "extra" parts is so elaborately developed as to exceed the interest of the assertion itself. The lawn (or shawl), for example, is not merely placed casually about the shoulders, but it is "thrown into a fine distraction"; the lace is not simply placed loosely around the stomacher, but it is "erring" and "enthralls" the stomacher; and so on.

Notice further that the second line explains exactly why the speaker admires casual dress. This is a structural part, for the reader is given thereby to understand that the speaker delights in disorder because it suggests wantonness, and thus the very nature of that delight is made more precise.

The order, furthermore, helps Herrick make his point more vividly and delightfully. The overall sequence is subject-reason-examples-predicate, and as such is good exposition. But notice that the examples themselves follow a spatial order, from top to bottom: shoulders, midriff, wrist, ankles, feet. In being thus specific pictorially, Herrick both makes clearer what he means and conveys a sense of that merry triviality which is essential to the poem's affective power. This effect is reinforced, finally, by the fact that these five examples are given ten lines out of a total of fourteen.

Again manner is seen as making a certain context actual and as vivid as possible in its effect upon the reader.

poems for study and discussion ⋘⋘

In assignments made from the following poems, after understanding the language and defining the context, its unity, and its affective powers as suggested in the four preceding chapters, your problem is to show how the handling of that context puts it before the reader in an intelligible, clear, moving, and economical way. Your topics are point of view, selection, scale, and order.

THE PASSIONATE SHEPHERD TO HIS LOVE ⋘⋘ *Christopher Marlowe*

Come live with me and be my love,
And we will all the pleasures prove
That valleys, groves, hills, and fields,
Woods, or steepy mountain yields.

And we will sit upon the rocks,
Seeing the shepherds feed their flocks,
By shallow rivers, to whose falls
Melodious birds sing madrigals.

And I will make thee beds of roses,
And a thousand fragrant posies,
A cap of flowers, and a kirtle
Embroider'd all with leaves of myrtle.

A gown made of the finest wool,
Which from our pretty lambs we pull,
Fair linèd slippers for the cold,
With buckles of the purest gold.

A belt of straw and ivy buds
With coral clasps and amber studs:
And if these pleasures may thee move,
Come live with me and be my love.

The shepherd swains shall dance and sing
For thy delight each May-morning:
If these delights thy mind may move,
Then live with me and be my love.

THE NYMPH'S REPLY TO THE SHEPHERD ❮❮❮ *Sir Walter Ralegh*

If all the world and love were young,
And truth in every shepherd's tongue,
These pretty pleasures might me move
To live with thee and be thy Love.

Time drives the flocks from field to fold,
When rivers rage and rocks grow cold,
And Philomel becometh dumb;
The rest complains of cares to come.

The flowers do fade, and wanton fields
To wayward winter reckoning yields;
A honey tongue, a heart of gall,
Is fancy's spring, but sorrow's fall.

Thy gowns, thy shoes, thy beds of roses,
Thy cap, thy kirtle, and thy posies
Soon break, soon wither, soon forgotten,—
In folly ripe, in reason rotten.

Thy belt of straw and ivy buds,
Thy coral clasps and amber studs,
All these in me no means can move
To come to thee and be thy love.

But could youth last and love still breed,
Had joys no date nor age no need,
Then these delights my mind might move
To live with thee and be thy love.

THE BAIT ⋘ *John Donne*

Come live with me, and be my love,
And we will some new pleasures prove
Of golden sands, and crystal brooks,
With silken lines, and silver hooks.

There will the river whispering run
Warmed by thy eyes, more than the sun.
And there th' enamoured fish will stay,
Begging themselves they may betray.

When thou wilt swim in that live bath,
Each fish, which every channel hath,
Will amorously to thee swim,
Gladder to catch thee, than thou him.

If thou, to be so seen, beest loath,
By sun or moon, thou dark'nest both;
And if myself have leave to see,
I need not their light, having thee.

Let others freeze with angling reeds,
And cut their legs with shells and weeds,
Or treacherously poor fish beset
With strangling snare, or windowy net.

Let coarse bold hands from slimy nest
The bedded fish in banks out-wrest,
Or curious traitors, sleave-silk flies,
Bewitch poor fishes' wand'ring eyes.

For thee, thou need'st no such deceit,
For thou thyself art thine own bait;
That fish that is not catched thereby,
Alas, is wiser far than I.

HOW SOON HATH TIME ≪← *John Milton*

How soon hath Time the subtle thief of youth,
Stoln on his wing my three and twentieth year!
My hasting days fly on with full career,
But my late spring no bud or blossom shew'th.
Perhaps my semblance might deceive the truth,
That I to manhood am arriv'd so near,
And inward ripeness doth much less appear,
That some more timely-happy spirits indu'th.
Yet be it less or more, or soon or slow,
It shall be still in strictest measure ev'n,
To that same lot, however mean or high,
Toward which Time leads me, and the will of Heav'n;
All is, if I have grace to use it so,
As ever in my great task Master's eye.

TWENTY-FOUR YEARS ⋘ *Dylan Thomas*

Twenty-four years remind the tears of my eyes.
(Bury the dead for fear that they walk to the grave in labour.)
In the groin of the natural doorway I crouched like a tailor
Sewing a shroud for a journey
By the light of the meat-eating sun.
Dressed to die, the sensual strut begun,
With my red veins full of money,
In the final direction of the elementary town
I advance for as long as forever is.

SPRING AND FALL: TO A YOUNG CHILD ⋘ *Gerard Manley Hopkins*

Márgarét, are you gríeving
Over Goldengrove unleaving?
Leáves, líke the things of man, you
With your fresh thoughts care for, can you?
Ah! ás the heart grows older
It will come to such sights colder
By and by, nor spare a sigh
Though worlds of wanwood leafmeal lie;
And yet you wíll weep and know why.
Now no matter, child, the name:
Sórrow's spríngs áre the same.
Nor mouth had, no nor mind, expressed
What heart heard of, ghost guessed:
It ís the blight man was born for,
It is Margaret you mourn for.

TO A YOUNG GIRL ⋘
William Butler Yeats

My dear, my dear, I know
More than another
What makes your heart beat so;
Not even your own mother
Can know it as I know,
Who broke my heart for her
When the wild thought,
That she denies
And has forgot,
Set all her blood astir
And glittered in her eyes.

A NOISELESS PATIENT SPIDER   ⋘   *Walt Whitman*

A noiseless patient spider,
I mark'd where on a little promontory it stood isolated,
Mark'd how to explore the vacant vast surrounding,
It launched forth filament, filament, filament, out of itself,
Ever unreeling them, ever tirelessly speeding them.

And you O my soul where you stand,
Surrounded, detached, in measureless oceans of space,
Ceaselessly musing, venturing, throwing, seeking the spheres
    to connect them,
Till the bridge you will need be form'd, till the ductile anchor
    hold,
Till the gossamer thread you fling catch somewhere, O my soul.

DESIGN ⋘ *Robert Frost*

I found a dimpled spider, fat and white,
On a white heal-all, holding up a moth
Like a white piece of rigid satin cloth—
Assorted characters of death and blight
Mixed ready to begin the morning right,
Like the ingredients of a witches' broth—
A snow-drop spider, a flower like froth,
And dead wings carried like a paper kite.

What had that flower to do with being white,
The wayside blue and innocent heal-all?
What brought the kindred spider to that height,
Then steered the white moth thither in the night?
What but design of darkness to appall?—
If design govern in a thing so small.

SUNDAY MORNING ⋘ *Louis MacNeice*

Down the road someone is practicing scales,
The notes like little fishes vanish with a wink of tails,
Man's heart expands to tinker with his car
For this is Sunday morning, Fate's great bazaar;
Regard these means as ends, concentrate on this Now,
And you may grow to music or drive beyond Hindhead anyhow,
Take corners on two wheels until you go so fast
That you can clutch a fringe or two of the windy past,
That you can abstract this day and make it to the week of time
A small eternity, a sonnet self-contained in rhyme.

But listen, up the road, something gulps, the church spire
Opens its eight bells out, skulls' mouths which will not tire
To tell how there is no music or movement which secures
Escape from the weekday time. Which deadens and endures.

THE DOME OF SUNDAY ⋘ *Karl Shapiro*

With focus sharp as Flemish-painted face
In film of varnish brightly fixed
And through a polished hand-lens deeply seen,
Sunday at noon through hyaline thin air
Sees down the street,
And in the camera of my eye depicts
Row-houses and row-lives:
Glass after glass, door after door the same,
Face after face the same, the same,
The brutal visibility the same;

As if one life emerging from one house
Would pause, a single image caught between
Two facing mirrors where vision multiplies
Beyond perspective,
A silent clatter in the high-speed eye
Spinning out photo-circulars of sight.

I see slip to the curb the long machines
Out of whose warm and windowed rooms pirouette
Shellacked with silk and light
The hard legs of our women.
Our women are one woman, dressed in black.
The carmine printed mouth

And cheeks as soft as muslin-glass belong
Outright to one dark dressy man,
Merely a swagger at her curvy side.

This is their visit to themselves:
All day from porch to porch they weave
A nonsense pattern through the even glare,
Stealing in surfaces
Cold vulgar glances at themselves.

And high up in the heated room all day
I wait behind the plate glass pane for one,
Hot as a voyeur for a glimpse of one,
The vision to blot out this woman's sheen;
All day my sight records expensively
Row-houses and row-lives.

But nothing happens; no diagonal
With melting shadow falls across the curb:
Neither the blinded negress lurching through fatigue,
Nor exiles bleeding from their pores,
Not that bright bomb slipped lightly from its rack
To splinter every silvered glass and crystal prism,
Witch-bowl and perfume bottle
And billion candle-power dressing-bulb,
No direct hit to smash the shatter-proof
And lodge at last the quivering needle
Clean in the eye of one who stands transfixed
In fascination of her brightness.

A SLUMBER DID MY SPIRIT
SEAL ⟪⟪ *William Wordsworth*

A slumber did my spirit seal;
   I had no human fears;
She seemed a thing that could not feel
   The touch of earthly years.

No motion has she now, no force;
   She neither hears nor sees;
Rolled round in earth's diurnal course,
   With rocks, and stones, and trees.

THE GOING ⟪⟪ *Thomas Hardy*

Why did you give no hint that night
That quickly after the morrow's dawn,
And calmly, as if indifferent quite,
You would close your term here, up and be gone
   Where I could not follow
   With wing of swallow
To gain one glimpse of you ever anon!

   Never to bid good-bye,
   Or lip me the softest call,
Or utter a wish for a word, while I
Saw morning harden upon the wall,
   Unmoved, unknowing
   That your great going
Had place that moment, and altered all.

Why do you make me leave the house
And think for a breath it is you I see
At the end of the alley of bending boughs
Where so often at dusk you used to be;
    Till in darkening dankness
    The yawning blankness
Of the perspective sickens me!

You were she who abode
    By those red-veined rocks far West,
You were the swan-necked one who rode
Along the beetling Beeny Crest,
    And, reining nigh me,
    Would muse and eye me,
While Life unrolled us its very best.

Why, then, latterly did we not speak,
Did we not think of those days long dead,
And ere your vanishing strive to seek
That time's renewal? We might have said,
    'In this bright spring weather
    We'll visit together
Those places that once we visited.'

Well, well! All's past amend,
    Unchangeable. It must go.
I seem but a dead man held on end
To sink down soon. . . . O you could not know
    That such swift fleeing
    No soul foreseeing—
Not even I—would undo me so!

8 ⟪⟪⟪ ask how the artistic purpose is served by style

In a certain sense, one of the poet's most pressing problems is his use of language, for the words he uses actually embody the poem for him as he writes it. Similarly, after he is finished, the words most immediately govern the impact of the poem upon the reader. The way something is said, therefore, helps to fashion both what is said and how it is to be taken.

A poem is made out of words, then, and so we are brought back to where we started in Chapter 3. But with a difference: in our chapter on meaning we considered words in terms of what they stood for, while here we must consider them in terms of their power to vivify the context through the use of auras of suggestion, sound effects, rhythm, and so on. They are something with surface as well as depth, something to look at as well as through, something with existence as well as reference. Language, this is to say, has two powers: to communicate meanings and to present a feeling-tone of its own. Naturally, a skillful writer will harness these powers together, but we can separate them for purposes of analysis. Indeed, it is only because they are separable that the critic can gauge the effectiveness of the poet's harnessing. A given experience, after all, exists as a conception in the poet's mind, and it could conceivably be embodied in a non-linguistic medium—as, for example, when what is narrated verbally in a novel is shown visually in a screen adaptation.

I

To analyze the *style* of poetry is a very complex affair, and we shall limit ourselves to the most basic topics: diction, sound, rhythm, and figures.

Diction refers to the poet's choice of words, among the available alternatives, in the service of a given effect. Two concepts are fundamental to the analysis of diction: first, that synonyms exist, and second, that they carry slightly different meanings. How to explain this difference? Words have histories and these histories cause them to be enveloped in growing and dying layers of subtly modulated meanings. According to the way a word has been used countless times over a span of hundreds of years, it will develop hosts of connotations, suggestions, and feelings beyond its specific or denotative meaning. And this process is interactive, for the way a word feels will effect the way it is used, and the way it is used will effect the way it feels. Take the word "skinny," for example, and compare it with such words as "thin" and "slender." The *denotation* of each is generally the same, but each has a different *connotation*. "Skinny" refers to a person who is unpleasantly thin, while "slender" refers to a person who is charmingly thin, and "thin" can go either way. Such differences aren't quite as crucial in speaking as they are in writing, for when one speaks one can produce the proper connotations by facial expression and tone of voice, but when one writes one must choose one's words with extreme care in order to convey the right impression.

These differences in connotative suggestion derive in large part from differences in usage, or the kinds of people and situations and tones with which certain words have become associated. Three general categories—loose but useful in their way —have been defined as a way of describing levels of usage: high or formal diction, middle or neutral diction, and low or informal diction. (A fourth category, technical diction or jargon, refers to the use of words taken from special studies and activities.) *Formal* diction is characterized by a preponderence of longer words derived from Latin and Greek or archaic English which are normally used on serious and elevated occasions or in literary writing—in the pulpit, for example, or the political rostrum. *Neutral* diction is standard English as it is spoken by people who want to be "correct" and yet not particularly elevated or literary—radio announcers, for example, or schoolteachers. *Informal* diction is the language used by nearly everyone when they are relaxing and talking to one another personally, and it is full of colloquialisms, loose constructions, and slang expressions. Since diction depends upon the occasion, no one kind of diction is "right" for all purposes—although poets writing as contemporaries often develop a characteristic poetic diction which they share in common. If you reflect a moment, you will recall that you naturally do not speak to your roommates in the same way that you speak to your parents, nor do you speak to your companion on a date in the same way that you speak to your friends in the locker room. The poet's choice of diction, then, is governed by the context he is working with and the effect he wants to create.

A second aspect of style is the poet's creation and disposition of *sounds*. It would be best not to make too much of this, for, although a poet can create beautiful effects by patterning his sounds, it is a very tenuous matter which frequently defies analysis. We shall, therefore, touch only upon the more obvious points. *Assonance* is created when words having similar vowel sounds are juxtaposed—in the "feeble reeds," for example, the long "e" sound is repeated. *Consonance* occurs when words having similar consonant sounds are juxtaposed—"terrible trouble," for example, repeats the "r" and "bl" sounds. When such repetitions occur at the beginning of two or more adjacent words, *alliteration* results—the "t" sound begins both words, for example, in "terrible trouble."

The most obvious use of sound patterns, however, is called *rhyme*. Rhyme is the repetition of at least one similar-sounding syllable at the end of at least two nearby lines. If a single syllable serves it is a *single rhyme* (song–wrong); if two a *double* (trouble–bubble); if three a *triple* (piety–anxiety). If the repeated sounds match it is a *full-rhyme* (love–dove); but if only part of the syllable is repeated, or if the repeated sounds are not precisely alike, then it is a *half-rhyme* (man–sun). A rhyming syllable which coincides with an accent is a *masculine rhyme* (alive–derive); one which falls on a slack syllable is a *feminine rhyme* (standing–handing). Repeated final syllables which fall within the line rather than at the end are *internal rhymes*.

Furthermore, rhymes may be used to form regular patterns of repeated final syllables and these patterns help to produce what are called *stanzas*. It is customary to indicate rhyming syllables with lower-case letters in alphabetical order, each rhymed syllable being assigned the same letter whenever it occurs in the poem. Rhymes falling into groups of two form *couplets*—aa bb cc dd; groups of three form *triplets* or *tercets* —aaa bbb ccc, or aba cbc dcd; groups of four form *quatrains* —abab, or abba, or aaba; groups of five form *quintains*; of six, *sestets*; of seven, *septets*; of eight, *octets*; and so on.

Certain stanzaic patterns have developed traditionally as fixed schemes for whole poems, the most common of which is the *sonnet*. The specifications of the sonnet include fourteen iambic pentameter lines (see p. 126) rhyming in fixed ways. An *Italian sonnet* rhymes abba abba cde cde (with certain variations), while an *English sonnet* rhymes ababcdcdefefgg (with certain variations). You will notice that the English scheme allows for more rhymes. This is probably because

rhyming sounds are more frequent in an inflected language such
as Italian than they are in English. Within the framework of
the sonnet the poet may subdivide the whole into two quatrains
and two tercets, or an octet and a sestet, or (in the English version) three quatrains and a couplet, and so on. It used to be
thought that there were certain "rules" prescribing how sonnets
should be written, but here as elsewhere poets have a way of
doing what they want and so many variations are possible as to
discredit the idea of absolute standards.

Other fixed stanzaic schemes—inherited mainly from medi-
eval and renaissance French and Italian poetry—are the bal-
lade, the villanelle, the rondel, the rondeau, the triolet, and the
sestina, among others. The details of these schemes are beyond
the scope of this book but they can be found in any standard
text on poetic meters and stanzas.

These devices of sound have many uses for creating the
proper effect of a poem: assonance and consonance may suggest
moods, for example, or imitate physical phenomena; alliteration
creates emphasis or imitates emotional states; rhyme creates
pleasure in itself and provides organizing and regularizing
patterns. None of these uses has any specific relevance, however,
apart from the meanings which the words convey.

Rhythm, a third aspect of style, is a repetition in time. English repeats *accented* syllables, and a syllable which is accented
is given relatively more force of utterance (not to be confused
with pitch or duration or volume) than its neighbors. *Meter* is
a special sort of rhythm in which the recurrence is regular, for
example, every other syllable accented, or every third. Each
stressed syllable along with its accompanying *slack syllables*
is called a *foot*. The meter of a line is described in terms of the
type of foot it uses and the number of feet in each line. An
iambic foot has a slack syllable followed by a stressed syllable
(ălóne); a *trochaic* has a stressed followed by a slack (dáintў);

an *anapestic* has two slacks followed by a stress (vǐllǎnélle); a *dactylic* has a strcssed followed by two slacks (délǐcǎte). One foot per line is called *monometer*, two *dimeter*, three *trimeter*, four *tetrameter*, five *pentameter*, six *hexameter*, seven *heptameter*, and so on. Thus a given line may use iambic pentameter, or trochaic tetrameter, or other combinations.

Poets are rarely content, and properly so, to write in perfectly regular meters, and certain *variations* have been introduced which we must now touch upon. One sort of variation is to make one or more feet in the line differ from the standard pattern—for example, a trochaic foot in an iambic line. A second sort of variation is to play the felt *rhetorical stress* of the utterance against the meter—as when the meter calls for emphasis on a syllable which would not normally be stressed ("Aňd óthěrs' feét stǐll séemed bǔt strángěrs iń mў wáy"). A third type of variation is to add an extra slack syllable at the end of a line which should normally end in a stress, or to increase the number of slack syllables throughout the line above their regular number, or to place slack syllables out of their regular order so that stressed syllables come together (these last two variations make up what Hopkins called *sprung rhythm:* "Nŏw, léavěd hŏw thíck! lácěd thěў aŕe ǎgáin"). A fourth is to vary the placement of *pauses,* either within the lines or at the end. A line which has a pause at its end is called *endstopped,* and one which has no end-pause is called *run-on.*

What are the uses of meter? There are many. Intenser emotions may be suggested, for example, by regular rhythms, for meters can be slow or rapid, heavy or light, tripping or ponderous, and these effects have in general certain emotional associations. Or again, meter serves to distinguish poetry from the language of common speech in giving it a magical and incantatory flavor and making it thereby more pleasing and memorable. A pattern of rhythmic regularity, like rhyme, set ups expectations in the reader which the poet can manipulate in the service of his effect. It also helps him create emphases, pauses, movements, in relation to meaning. Meter also creates pressures which he must control: the choice of a metrical pattern is for the poet something of voluntary contract between himself and the poem, a commitment, and part of his skill is shown in how well he brings this commitment into line with all his other commitments in the poem. If he succeeds, then the pattern of rhythm which he sets up will help him render the various aspects of his context more effectively—intensity, compactness, and a sense of order are the result.

But none of this is strictly necessary, for a poet may use meters badly and fail to achieve these effects, or he may dispense with meter and succeed. *Free verse,* or poetic rhythm without meter and rhyme, is a controversial and complicated subject, but we must at least mention it here. Poets for at least the past hundred years have been consciously searching for principles of rhythmic regularity other than the metrical, and their findings have been viewed as shredded prose by hostile critics and as new directions by favorable ones. The problem of the experimental poet is to avoid the obvious, the mechanical, the ordinary, and to achieve more subtlety in his effects, make them more functional, more striking. This he attempts by setting up patterns of cadences (based on the rhythm of the phrase rather than the stress of syllables), repetitions and variations in syntactical structures, schemes of images, and so on.

All of which borders on considerations appropriate to the fourth element of style—*figures.* This term refers to various artful elaborations of style and includes figures of language, figures of thought, and figures of speech.

Figures of language involve phrasal and syntactical patterns. Two or more adjacent phrases or clauses having a similar syntactical structure form a *balance;* if these units express similar meanings they form a *parallelism,* if opposite meanings they form an *antithesis.* "Ye who listen with credulity to the whispers of fancy, and pursue with eagerness the phantoms of hope" is an example of a parallelism, while "art is long but life is short" is an example of an antithesis. An *inversion* results when the normal word order of a clause is changed in some manner, as in "With rue my heart is laden" instead of "My heart is laden with rue." A series of short coordinate clauses without other expression of their syntactic relation is called *parataxis,* as in "I came; I saw; I conquered." *Hypotaxis,* on the other hand, refers to clauses with expressed subordinate relations. A *periodic* sentence or clause is one in which there is much subordination in the middle, with the main clause being completed only at the end. And there are many other such devices with difficult Greek or Latin names, but we shall content ourselves with merely having given you the basic idea involved in figures of language. Their uses are in general to give force and distinction to style, to help achieve emphasis, to suggest moods or feelings.

Figures of thought are ways of expressing a meaning in an unusual fashion. A *pun,* for example, is the use of a single word with two or more denotations, or of two different words which sound alike, in such a way that various meanings are played off against one another. The word "stable," for example, refers as a noun to a shed for horses and as an adjective to a degree of steadiness; "sea" and "see," for example, are different words which happen to sound alike. *Irony* is found in an expression which says one thing but really means its opposite, as when one says "I had *some* fun!" in common parlance but really means "I had a rather difficult time." A *paradox* results when one says something which is apparently contradictory or which is contrary to accepted ideas—"the flesh is spiritual," for example, or "April is the cruellest month." *Hyperbole* is deliberate exaggeration for effect, as when a lover claims that his lady is "a resplendent goddess," or that he "dies" when he is absent from her. *Litotes*, or calculated understatement, is the reverse of hyperbole, for it deliberately minimizes for effect, as when a person says after an intensely delightful experience that "it was all right." A *periphrasis* expresses an idea in more elevated or round-about terms than is customary, as in "passing away" for "dying," for example, or "entering the holy estate of matrimony" for "getting married." An *ellipsis* is the opposite of periphrasis, for it expresses an idea in an unusually short and bare manner, as in "principles I believe" for "the principles which I believe in."

Again, we have given you only the barest outlines of a complex matter. Enough has been said, however, to give you an idea of what such devices are and how they may be used to emphasize, or surprise, or reinforce attitudes.

Figures of speech, finally, have to do with departures from a literal and direct manner of expression. A figure of speech compares or identifies two things which are normally considered to be different, and thus involves, as we suggested in our third chapter, a subject, an analogue, and an analogy. In using a figurative expression instead of a literal statement of his subject, the poet achieves many things: he makes clearer the precise way in which he wants his subject to be taken, he imports into the statement a host of suggestive associations by means of the analogue, and he makes his expression more vivid and tangible. It is important to remember, however, in interpreting figures of speech, to develop the analogy in terms of the context of the poem as a whole, for going too far will break down a figure and make it disruptive.

The various sorts of subject-analogue relationships are defined as follows. A *simile* compares them explicitly—"troubles are like" or "as a sea," for example. The analogy here has to do with the way one feels when one is bathing in a pounding

surf or adrift in a tempestuous ocean storm, namely, over-
whelmed, dizzy, suffocated, lost, in danger, helpless, despairing,
as one feels when troubles come thick and fast. A *metaphor*
identifies them implicitly, as in "a sea of troubles." Here the
connection between the subject (troubles) and the analogue
(sea) is implicit, but notice that the analogy is left to inference
here as well as in the simile. In *personification* the subject is
something nonhuman—whether a thing, a creature, or idea—
and the analogue is some human trait, quality, power, or attribute, as when the sea "moans" or when troubles "tyrannize."
An *allegory* is an experience or story in which the characters
are personified abstractions, and the physical events and places
stand for something in a pattern of ideas. A *symbol* involves
an analogue so treated and developed as to suggest its subject
without that subject itself being mentioned, as when a poet
writes of a sea journey in such a way as to imply that he is
speaking of his troubles. In a *synecdoche* the analogue is a
part of the subject and is said in its place, or a whole of which
the subject is a part, or a container in which the subject is
contained, and so on for cause and effect and other similar relationships, as when one says a certain hostess "sets a good
table," meaning she serves good meals (container is substituted
for thing contained). In *metonymy* an analogue is put in the
place of a subject with which it has a common association, as
when one says "the Cross" for Christianity.

II

It remains to illustrate how these principles and powers of
style may be seen working in a poem. At this point it will suffice
if we work only with "Desert Places," both for the sake of
economy as well as for the reason that the elements of stylistic
analysis are not fundamentally different, as far as this book is
concerned, for different sorts of poems.

Frost's diction in this poem is primarily neutral shading into colloquial or informal; and it is one of his special achievements to have developed such an apparently casual idiom for the treatment of highly imaginative, emotional, and thoughtful states. The few variations here are "benighted" and "ere" in the direction of formal, and the word "scare" in the direction of informal diction. By and large Frost creates in this poem a certain kind of man as his protagonist and his stylistic problem is to suit the word to the deed. Thus, since his speaker is an imaginative yet realistic sort of person, his diction is neutral touched with formal as well as informal elements: this man is not going to be carried away by his emotions, nor is he going to plod along in one dull routine, but rather will respond to life perceptively while at the same time keeping a firm grip on himself. If Frost had had him say, for example, "Snow descending and night descending rapidly ah rapidly" instead of "Snow falling and night falling fast oh fast," he would have been putting before the reader a different sort of man in a different sort of mood. That is because our revision is more formal, suggesting a more self-conscious and calculating person and feeling, and giving the impression of a reaction both more inflated and more detached. As Frost wrote the line, a sense of bare, cold, swift movement is conveyed, along with a sense of a man engaged in and directly affected by this movement.

Similar analyses of the rest of the poem's diction in terms of the seriousness of the experience being portrayed and the emotions of sympathy and pity being aimed at will be reserved for class discussion. Let us now turn to Frost's sound patterns. Notice, for example, the alliteration of "f" sounds in the first line, which serves to emphasize and bind together the key words in the line. Notice the consonance created in the eighth line by the recurrence of "n" sounds, which helps suggest the feeling of numbness which the speaker feels. Notice the assonance created in the eleventh line by the repetition of the long "i" sound in "whiteness" and "benighted," which helps to create the atmosphere of ghostly blankness working on the speaker's mind so profoundly. The modulation of assonantal patterns may also be noticed in the third line, which moves from "ow" in "ground," to "oh" in "almost," to "uh" in "covered," to "oo" in "smooth," and back to "oh" in "snow," which helps to suggest the 'smothering effect of the scene as a whole.

The rhyme scheme of the poem forms quatrains, and they rhyme aaba ccdc eebe ffgf. They are all full masculine rhymes and are all single, except the f-rhyme which is double as well as feminine, creating thereby an appropriate falling effect at the end. Beyond this, all that need be said here is that this pattern helps Frost make symmetrical the various phases of the experience which he is portraying and helps him to create expectations to be resolved gradually throughout. This neatness adds a touch of formality to the poem which offsets slightly the neutrality of the diction.

The meter is basically iambic pentameter, with variations. The seventh line is relatively regular:

A blan|ker white|ness of|benight|ed snow

As you can see, there are five feet and each one is an iamb. The first line, however, illustrates certain variations:

Snow fall|ing and night|falling|fast|oh fast

There are still five feet but they are not all iambs. The first is an iamb with a rhetorical or hovering accent over the first syllable, the second is an anapest, the third is a trochee, the fourth is a single stressed syllable, and the fifth is an iamb. Again, there are slight pauses after the two "fallings" as well as at the end of the line. All of which serves to emphasize the key words and syllables creating the ghostly mood. Notice that the ninth line is run-on, that the thirteenth and fourteenth and sixteenth lines have an extra slack syllable at the end, and so on.

The first line will also illustrate Frost's handling of balance and parallelism:

> snow falling
>   and
> night falling
>
> fast
>   oh
> fast

This pattern creates a lovely sense of the eeriness of the scene in repeating similar words and phrases adjacently. The point could perhaps be made more clearly if we kept the same words but rearranged their sequence, as in "Snow falling fast and oh night falling fast":

> snow falling fast
>   and
>   oh
> night falling fast

It is still balanced and parallel but it does not repeat twice, as does the original, and it is this repetition which creates the proper emphasis. It is as if the night and the snow in the original were more "falling" and more "fast" by virtue of this repetitive parallelism. You may wish to examine the other syntactical patterns in this poem—especially the wonderful way in which "lonely" and "loneliness," "no expression" and "nothing to express" are handled in the third stanza.

There are no figures of thought to speak of here, but something remains to be said about figures of speech. While snow can literally fall, night cannot. "Night falling" is certainly not a particularly unusual metaphor, however, being by now used in common parlance almost literally. Such expressions are called *fossil* or *radical metaphors* because, although they may have been figurative at one time, they no longer have that force. And language is full of them: "spirit," for example, once meant breath; "metaphor" has as its root meaning to carry over or transfer; "enlighten" comes from a meaning having to do with physical light. The poet's job is to re-awaken these fossils in his verse, which is precisely what Frost does here. Night can literally happen, or come, or arrive, but when one says it falls one means that darkness seems to "come down" in the sense of being a covering or lid in relation to the earth. Also, one means that the sun, in passing beyond the western horizon, seems to drop out of the sky and therefore to drag night along after it. Associated with these feelings is a feeling of sinking, of dropping, and consequently of being swallowed up or covered over. The point is that one usually doesn't have a glimmer of these connotations in one's mind when one says "night is falling" in ordinary speech, but that Frost awakens them by placing the fossil in a context wherein his speaker is having exactly these feelings and ideas. Part of this awakening process begins by placing the expression in close conjunction with the literal expression "Snow falling," for this can be seen and felt and consequently helps the reader to see and feel similar things regarding night falling which he would not otherwise notice.

There is some personification in lines five and eight having to do with moods and loneliness, and a common but again curiously suggestive metaphor at the end in "nearer home." The most important figure of the poem, however, results from the cumulative associations with which the speaker's reflection surrounds the scene itself, and may be called a symbol. Although the scene exists in its own right as a literal physical presence to which the speaker responds (symbolic images may also be imaginary or invented), so much thought and feeling are poured into it that it serves as an analogue of those thoughts and feelings by the end of the poem. The crucial thing about the scene which impresses the speaker, as we have shown, is its blankness and lack of expression, and when this is related in the last stanza to cosmic emptiness, and when both of these are associated with the spiritual emptiness within the speaker's soul, then it may be said that the scene symbolizes spiritual desolation. Thus the image of "desert places" refers at once to the empty field, the spaces between stars, and the speaker's inner emptiness. But beware of over-interpreting such a device: make sure, first, that a literal interpretation won't suffice, and, second, that the meanings you trace out are suggested by the context and not by mere ingenuity.

After covering the analytical steps discussed in the five preceding chapters on meaning, context, unity, artistic purpose, and technique, as they apply to poems assigned from the following group, you are now to discuss the devices of language and to show how they relate to the poem as a whole. Your topics are diction, sound, rhythm, and figures.

AND WILT THOU LEAVE ME THUS? ⋘ *Sir Thomas Wyatt*

And wilt thou leave me thus?
  Say nay, say nay! For shame!
  To save thee from the blame
  Of all my grief and grame.
And wilt thou leave me thus?
  Say nay, say nay.

And wilt thou leave me thus,
  That hath loved thee so long
  In wealth and woe among?
  And is thy heart so strong
As for to leave me thus?
  Say nay, say nay.

And wilt thou leave me thus,
  That hath given thee my heart,
  Never for to depart
  Neither for pain nor smart;
And wilt thou leave me thus?
  Say nay, say nay.

149

And wilt thou leave me thus,
And have no more pity
Of him that loveth thee?
Alas, thy cruelty!
And wilt thou leave me thus?
Say nay, say nay!

LOVING IN TRUTH ⋘ *Sir Philip Sidney*

Loving in truth, and fain in verse my love to show,
That she, dear she, might take some pleasure of my pain,
Pleasure might cause her read, reading might make her know,
Knowledge might pity win, and pity grace obtain,—
I sought fit words to paint the blackest face of woe;
Studying inventions fine, her wits to entertain,
Oft turning others' leaves to see if thence would flow
Some fresh and fruitful showers upon my sun-burned brain.
But words came halting forth, wanting invention's stay;
Invention, nature's child, fled step-dame Study's blows,
And others' feet still seemed but strangers in my way.
Thus, great with child to speak, and helpless in my throes,
Biting my truant pen, beating myself for spite,
Fool, said my muse to me, look in thy heart and write.

SINCE THERE'S NO HELP, COME LET US KISS AND PART ⋘ *Michael Drayton*

Since there's no help, come let us kiss and part.
Nay, I have done, you get no more of me,
And I am glad, yea, glad with all my heart
That thus so cleanly I myself can free;
Shake hands for ever, cancel all our vows,
And when we meet at any time again,

Be it not seen in either of our brows
    That we one jot of former love retain.
Now at the last gasp of Love's latest breath,
    When, his pulse failing, Passion speechless lies,
When Faith is kneeling by his bed of death,
    And Innocence is closing up his eyes,
            Now if thou wouldst, when all have given him over,
            From death to life thou mightst him yet recover.

TO DAFFODILS   *Robert Herrick*

Fair daffodils, we weep to see
    You haste away so soon;
As yet the early-rising sun
    Has not attained his noon.
            Stay, stay,
        Until the hasting day
            Has run
        But to the even-song;
And, having prayed together, we
    Will go with you along.

We have short time to stay, as you;
    We have as short a spring,
As quick a growth to meet decay,
    As you, or anything.
            We die
        As hours do, and dry
            Away
Like to the summer's rain,
Or as the pearls of morning's dew,
    Ne'er to be found again.

THE RETREAT ⋘
Henry Vaughan

Happy those early days when I
Shin'd in my angel-infancy!
Before I understood this place
Appointed for my second race,
Or taught my soul to fancy aught
But a white, celestial thought;
When yet I had not walkt above
A mile or two from my first love,
And looking back at that short space,
Could see a glimpse of His bright face;
When on some gilded cloud or flower,
My gazing soul would dwell an hour,
And in those weaker glories spy
Some shadows of eternity;
Before I taught my tongue to wound
My conscious with a sinful sound,
Or had the black art to dispense
A sev'ral sin to ev'ry sense;
But felt through all this fleshly dress
Bright shoots of everlastingness.
    O how I long to travel back
And tread again that ancient track!
That I might once more reach that plain
Where first I left my glorious train,
From whence th' enlightened spirit sees
That shady City of Palm Trees.
But, ah! my soul with too much stay,
Is drunk, and staggers in the way.

Some men a forward motion love,
But I by backward steps would move,
And when this dust falls to the urn,
In that state I came return.

ODE ON SOLITUDE   *Alexander Pope*

Happy the man, whose wish and care
A few paternal acres bound,
Content to breathe his native air,
    In his own ground.

Whose herds with milk, whose fields with bread,
Whose flocks supply him with attire,
Whose trees in summer yield him shade,
    In winter, fire.

Blest, who can unconcernedly find
Hours, days, and years slide soft away,
In health of body, peace of mind,
    Quiet by day,

Sound sleep by night; study and ease,
Together mixed; sweet recreation;
And innocence, which most does please,
    With meditation.

Thus let me live, unseen, unknown,
Thus unlamented let me die,
Steal from the world, and not a stone
    Tell where I lie.

TO SPRING ⋘ *William Blake*

O, thou with dewy locks, who lookest down
Thro' the clear windows of the morning, turn
Thine angel eyes upon our western isle,
Which in full choir hails thy approach, O Spring!

The hills tell each other, and the list'ning
Valleys hear; all our longing eyes are turned
Up to thy bright pavillions: issue forth,
And let thy holy feet visit our clime.

Come o'er the eastern hills, and let our winds
Kiss thy perfumed garments; let us taste
Thy morn and evening breath; scatter thy pearls
Upon our love-sick land that mourns for thee.

O, deck her forth with thy fair fingers; pour
Thy soft kisses on her bosom; and put
Thy golden crown upon her languished head,
Whose modest tresses were bound up for thee!

I AM ⋘ *John Clare*

I am: yet what I am none cares or knows,
     My friends forsake me like a memory lost;
I am the self-consumer of my woes,
     They rise and vanish in oblivious host,
Like shades in love and death's oblivion lost;
And yet I am, and live with shadows tost

Into the nothingness of scorn and noise,
   Into the living sea of waking dreams,
Where there is neither sense of life nor joys,
   But the vast shipwreck of my life's esteems;
And e'en the dearest—that I loved the best—
Are strange—nay, rather stranger than the rest.

I long for scenes where man has never trod,
   A place where woman never smiled or wept;
There to abide with my Creator, God,
   And sleep as I in childhood sweetly slept:
Untroubling and untroubled where I lie,
The grass below—above the vaulted sky.

THE SONNET   ❰❰❰   *Dante Gabriel Rossetti*

A Sonnet is a moment's monument,—
   Memorial from the Soul's eternity
   To one dead deathless hour. Look that it be,
Whether for lustral rite or dire portent,
Of its own arduous fullness reverent:
   Carve it in ivory or in ebony,
   As Day or Night may rule; and let Time see
Its flowering crest impearled and orient.

A Sonnet is a coin: its face reveals
   The soul,—its converse, to what Power 'tis due:—
Whether for tribute to the august appeals
   Of Life, or dower in Love's high retinue,
It serve; or, 'mid the dark wharf's cavernous breath,
In Charon's palm it pay the toll to Death.

A COAT ⋘ *William Butler Yeats*

I made my song a coat
Covered with embroideries
Out of old mythologies
From heel to throat;
But the fools caught it,
Wore it in the world's eyes
As though they'd wrought it.
Song, let them take it,
For there's more enterprise
In walking naked.

DEAD BOY ⋘ *John Crowe Ransom*

The little cousin is dead, by foul subtraction,
A green bough from Virginia's aged tree,
And none of the county kin like the transaction,
Nor some of the world of outer dark, like me.

A boy not beautiful, nor good, nor clever,
A black cloud full of storms too hot for keeping,
A sword beneath his mother's heart—yet never
Woman bewept her babe as this is weeping.

A pig with a pasty face, so I had said,
Squealing for cookies, kinned by poor pretense
With a noble house. But the little man quite dead,
I see the forebears' antique lineaments.

The elder men have strode by the box of death
To the wide flag porch, and muttering low send round

The bruit of the day. O friendly waste of breath!
Their hearts are hurt with a deep dynastic wound.

He was pale and little, the foolish neighbors say;
The first-fruits, saith the Preacher, the Lord hath taken;
But this was the old tree's late branch wrenched away,
Grieving the sapless limbs, the shorn and shaken.

HOW SHALL I EVER COME TO ANY
GOOD? ≪← *Winfield Townley Scott*

How shall I ever come to any good
And get my works in schoolbooks if I use
A rough word here and there, but how shall I
Let you know me if I bequeath you only
The several photographs, the family letters?

There is no image of a tired mind
Tired of its own vanity for fame.
I turn in the comfort of the midnight rain
And as much for pleasure as necessity
Piss in the river beyond O'Ryan's bar.

9 ⋘ test your conception of the whole poem

Have we by now achieved an organizing conception of "Desert Places," that sense of the whole which we set out to look for at the beginning of this book? Recall that a sense of the whole involves seeing how the four aspects of the making of a poem are related—material, manner, shape, and end. Recall further how we argued that each of these parts must be related to the others hierarchically if a whole is to result. Up to now we have been discussing that relationship from the point of view of the reader: the affective powers of a poem are determined by the way in which its context is conceived and unified, the manner in which it is handled, and the kind of language in which it is embodied. Determined, that is to say, from the point of view of the reader who is trying to infer, on the basis of the completed work, what its organizing principle is. The concept of hierarchical determination, however, can be regarded from the poet's point of view as he tries to weld all the aspects of his work into a completed work: the impression he wants to make on the reader will tell him how his context should be conceived and unified. This conception will in turn tell him how that context should be handled, and all of these things will tell him in turn what sort of language to use.

The reader in search of a gestalt, then, will arrive on the basis of the completed poem at a notion of what its affective powers are and how these are produced and made vivid by the context, the techniques, and the language. Next, he will postulate or hypothesize that these affective powers are the determining principle of the work and will go on in an effort to re-think the poet's problems in those terms. This *hypothesis* offers a reasoning principle, without which the reader cannot understand why the poet did what he did. And if it does explain all the poet's choices in terms of one principle, then it may be assumed that a gestalt has been reached.

But there are better and worse hypotheses and we must now explain how to tell the difference. In the first place, since the proper interpretation of poems is a delicate matter, you must get into the habit of systematically considering alternative hypotheses. Interpretation in any field of study depends upon two things: establishing the evidence and finding ways of explaining its significance. In literary study, unlike that of the exact sciences, the evidence (what is said in a work and how it is said) cannot finally be measured with mechanical precision, nor does the explanation (how the work is organized) aim at formulating general laws. In interpreting a poem the reader is thrown back upon his knowledge, taste, and skill, and he seeks not an explanation of poetry in general but an increased awareness of the poem itself in all its vivid particularity. Thus no one interpretation can be demonstrated once and for all to be the whole and complete truth about a poem.

This does not mean, however, that it's every reader for himself. In relation to what the words of a poem *can* mean and how they *may* be organized, there are more and less plausible interpretations. Readers can compare interpretations, in other words, and they can reason about their comparisons, choosing among them on the basis of which one answers the particular question under discussion most satisfactorily. The best hypothesis, then, is the best only in relation to the other possibilities; it is hardly a question of "right" or "wrong," but of better and worse. That is why you must consider the alternatives. Even if you are doing well to begin with, you won't be able to appreciate why you are doing well unless you give other theories a chance to be heard. And if you are not doing well, you may be brought out of your impasse by asking for comparisons. Indeed, error in this case (as in so many others) is positively educative, for no better way of coming to an adequate answer can be found than by discussing and testing the inadequate ones first.

A moment's recollection will make clear to you, if it is not already obvious, that we have been following such a method all along in this book. For example, in Chapter 3, when we discussed the meaning of Hopkins' "mean," we did so in terms of what the word *could* mean and which of these meanings *could* be applied to that word in the poem. In Chapter 4, when we explained the various sorts of contexts around which poems may be built, we offered three possibilities to consider. In asking what unified the experience presented in "Desert Places" in Chapter 5, we treated thought, character, and reaction in turn as possibilities. In discussing the artistic purpose of this poem in Chapter 6, we considered whether that experience was being presented for its own sake or for the sake of some idea or doctrine. And in explaining the uses of poetic techniques and stylistic devices in Chapters 7 and 8, we suggested a variety of principles for interpreting artistic choices of this kind.

But the problem still remains: once the alternatives have been raised, how is one to choose among them? How can you know which one answers the particular question under discussion most satisfactorily? If you don't have laboratories and gauges and meters, you do have rational principles to guide you. That hypothesis is most adequate which is most complete, most coherent, and most economical.

Regarding completeness, remember that there are four variables to consider in the definition of any given whole, and that therefore any hypothesis must attempt to cover them all. It may be, especially in larger poems, that all four cannot be held at once in the mind, so what you must do is to proceed one step at a time, hold the main determining principle of the work in mind throughout, and reach the end of your inquiry by cumulative stages. It is easy to explain many things in a poem if you ignore certain of its details or if you distort them to suit your hypothesis. Many different hypotheses may be fashioned to explain any single poem partially, but few can be found to explain it entirely; the range of possibilities narrows as your grasp of the evidence becomes more and more complete. If you find, after framing a theory, that another theory will fit the poem even better, then you had best look again at your evidence. Similarly, if you find that your theory will fit other and different poems equally well, then you had best suspect that something is wrong, for a whole is by definition distinctive. Get in the habit of looking for details in the poem which you haven't explained, for whatever is in the poem—whether suggested or stated—constitutes evidence: the context and the way it is conceived, the manner in which it is handled, and the language which is used. And try not to precondition your findings on the basis of a hypothesis you may have formed before thinking the poem through.

A theory which is consistent within itself so that all its parts are unified is said to be coherent. You cannot postulate about an ax, for example, that its cutting edge is at the head but that you are meant to chop with the handle. Your assumption that its cutting edge is at the head necessarily means that you must chop with the head.

And a theory, finally, which explains what it is designed to explain with the fewest additional and supplementary hypotheses is said to be economical. If you find yourself theorizing about the cutting edge of an ax by bringing in assumptions as to gravity and the rotation of the earth, you had best reconsider and see if you can explain it in a simpler and more direct fashion.

Having found, among the alternatives, what seems to be a reasonable hypothesis for explaining the organization of "Desert Places," let us test it for completeness, coherence, and economy. Does it explain all of the poet's choices (or almost all, for poets often surpass our powers of explanation) in terms of a single principle? This is not to say that any one element in a poem need have only one function, or that all of the elements need have the same function, but rather that all of the varied elements with all of their many functions may be seen as working, in the last analysis, toward a common goal.

How will our theory—that Frost's intention was to evoke compassion in the reader for a man who has been led to gaze upon his own innermost desolation—explain all that is done in the poem? Is this a principle without which we cannot explain all of the poet's choices? Before we try to answer this question, let us remind you that it has taken us many chapters to reach our hypothesis and that therefore you are not to be misled by the following paragraphs into thinking it came easily and without testing.

Ask first, in what light the experience seems to be conceived. Look at the poem for an answer: the speaker is alone, he is absent-spirited, it is dusk, it is snowing, he fails to find any expression in the scene, he is reminded of the dead spaces between stars, and concludes that his own desert places are more frightening. He is experiencing mental anguish and is in a heightened state of imaginative awareness. Why did Frost put the experience in this way? Because he wanted it to strike the reader as serious. Why did he have his speaker conclude on a note of intensified fear? Because he wanted to arouse the reader's pity. Why did he portray his protagonist as imaginative and perceptive? Because he wanted the reader to feel sympathetic.

Ask next about the manner in which this experience is handled.

Why is it told from the protagonist's present point of view? Because it places him inside the experience as the reader reads, and the reader can therefore most easily identify with him sympathetically. Why does the poem show the whole experience from beginning to end? Because, if the reader is to feel pity for the speaker's spiritual distress, he must be shown all the cumulative stages by which that distress is reached. Why is the experience compressed at the end? So that the reader will appreciate the full meaning and force of the climax of that evolving inner state. And why does the poem proceed chronologically? So that the reader will feel the development of this evolving inner state with maximum clarity and effect.

And the style. Why is the diction neutral? Because Frost wanted the reader to sense the true character of his protagonist. A more formal diction might have led the reader to question the immediacy and force of the speaker's mood, while a more informal diction might have led the reader to question the seriousness of the speaker's situation. Frost also wanted to recreate for the reader his speaker's ghostly and desolate mood by his choice of words. Why the sounds and rhymes? For the sake of the mood and its intensity. Why iambic pentameter rhythm? To heighten the emotional tone of the experience and to provide a line of sufficient amplitude for serious reflections. Why paralleled and balanced phrases? To emphasize the desolation and reinforce the fearful mood. Why personify the woods? To convey the speaker's feeling of being somehow menaced. Why is the scene as a whole a symbol? To vivify and make concrete the speaker's sense of his own inner desert places.

Can any other reason explain all these things? If not, then we have our gestalt. We have shown how a single principle may be used to explain why the experience is conceived in the way it is, how that conception explains the manner in which the experience is handled, and how that experience so conceived and handled explains why a certain kind of language is used. If no better reason is forthcoming, if this explanation is a consistent one, if it covers all the details of the poem, if nothing else is left over, and if all this is done economically, then we have the best available hypothesis. This is a relative matter, however, and we will always be on the lookout for a better way of explaining this poem. Even if we have missed something essential— and indeed many of the poet's choices rest upon such varied, particular, and minute grounds as to be beyond conscious formulation—we have succeeded in studying the poem from many angles, and in that study, we have come to know that poem more intimately than before.

We will not belabor the question with regard to "To Lose One's Faith" and "Delight in Disorder" beyond suggesting that the determining principle of the former is to be found in the author's attempts to move the reader's opinions in a certain way, and that the determining principle of the latter is to be found in the author's attempts to place a certain piece of information before the reader in a certain light. You may, if you wish, verify these hypotheses for yourselves.

poems for study and discussion ⫷⫷⫷

In assignments made from the following poems, your problem is to attempt a complete analysis of the meaning of the language, of the context containing this language, of the unity of this context, of its governing or shaping or affective principle, of its manner, and of its style. Then, after considering the alternatives, bring this analysis under the control of a complete, coherent, and economical hypothesis explaining the relationships among material, manner, context, and end.

POLITICS ⫷⫷⫷ *William Butler Yeats*

"In our time the destiny of man presents its meaning in political terms."
—THOMAS MANN

How can I, that girl standing there,
My attention fix
On Roman or on Russian
Or on Spanish politics?
Yet here's a travelled man that knows
What he talks about,
And there's a politician
That has read and thought,
And maybe what they say is true
Of war and war's alarms,
But O that I were young again
And held her in my arms!

WHO'S WHO ⟨⟨⟨   *W. H. Auden*

A shilling life will give you all the facts:
How Father beat him, how he ran away,
What were the struggles of his youth, what acts
Made him the greatest figure of his day:
Of how he fought, fished, hunted, worked all night,
Though giddy, climbed new mountains; named a sea:
Some of the last researchers even write
Love made him weep his pints like you and me.

With all his honors on, he sighed for one
Who, say astonished critics, lived at home;
Did little jobs about the house with skill
And nothing else; could whistle; would sit still
Or potter round the garden; answered some
Of his long marvellous letters, but kept none.

COULD MAN BE DRUNK FOR EVER ⟨⟨⟨   *A. E. Housman*

Could man be drunk for ever
    With liquor, love, or fights,
Lief should I rouse at morning
    And lief lie down of nights.

But men at whiles are sober
    And think by fits and starts,
And if they think, they fasten
    Their hands upon their hearts.

TO EARTHWARD ⋘   *Robert Frost*

Love at the lips was touch
As sweet as I could bear;
And once that seemed too much;
I lived on air

That crossed me from sweet things,
The flow of—was it musk
From hidden grapevine springs
Down hill at dusk?

I had the swirl and ache
From sprays of honeysuckle
That when they're gathered shake
Dew on the knuckle.

I craved strong sweets, but those
Seemed strong when I was young;
The petal of the rose
It was that stung.

Now no joy but lacks salt
That is not dashed with pain
And weariness and fault;
I crave the stain

Of tears, the aftermark
Of almost too much love,
The sweet of bitter bark
And burning clove.

When stiff and sore and scarred
I take away my hand
From leaning on it hard
In grass and sand,

The hurt is not enough:
I long for weight and strength
To feel the earth as rough
To all my length.

THE DARKLING THRUSH   ⋘   *Thomas Hardy*

I leant upon a coppice gate
    When Frost was spectre-gray,
And Winter's dregs made desolate
    The weakening eye of day.
The tangled bine-stems scored the sky
    Like strings of broken lyres,
And all mankind that haunted nigh
    Had sought their household fires.

The land's sharp features seemed to be
    The Century's corpse outleant,
His crypt the cloudy canopy,
    The wind his death-lament.
The ancient pulse of germ and birth
    Was shrunken hard and dry,
And every spirit upon earth
    Seemed fervourless as I.

At once a voice arose among
    The bleak twigs overhead

In a full-hearted evensong
    Of joy illimited;
An aged thrush, frail, gaunt, and small,
    In blast-beruffled plume,
Had chosen thus to fling his soul
    Upon the growing gloom.

So little cause for carolings
    Of such ecstatic sound
Was written on terrestrial things
    Afar or nigh around,
That I could think there trembled through
    His happy good-night air
Some blessed Hope, whereof he knew
    And I was unaware.

December 1900

THE DEATH OF THE BALL TURRET
GUNNER ⋘ *Randall Jarrell*

From my mother's sleep I fell into the State,
And I hunched in its belly till my wet fur froze.
Six miles from earth, loosed from its dream of life,
I woke to black flak and the nightmare fighters.
When I died they washed me out of the turret with a hose.

NEARING AGAIN THE LEGENDARY ISLE ⋘ *C. Day Lewis*

Nearing again the legendary isle
Where sirens sang and mariners were skinned,
We wonder now what was there to beguile
That such stout fellows left their bones behind.

Those chorus-girls are surely past their prime,
Voices grow shrill and paint is wearing thin,
Lips that sealed up the sense from gnawing time
Now beg the favour with a graveyard grin.

We have no flesh to spare and they can't bite,
Hunger and sweat have stripped us to the bone;
A skeleton crew we toil upon the tide
And mock the theme-song meant to lure us on:

No need to stop the ears, avert the eyes
From purple rhetoric of evening skies.

PIANO ⋘ *D. H. Lawrence*

Softly, in the dusk, a woman is singing to me;
Taking me back down the vista of years, till I see
A child sitting under the piano, in the boom of the tingling
  strings
And pressing the small, poised feet of a mother who smiles as
  she sings.

In spite of myself, the insidious mastery of song
Betrays me back, till the heart of me weeps to belong
To the old Sunday evenings at home, with winter outside
And hymns in the cozy parlour, the tinkling piano our guide.

So now it is vain for the singer to burst into clamour
With the great black piano appassionato. The glamour
Of childish days is upon me, my manhood is cast
Down in the flood of remembrance, I weep like a child for the
    past.

SALUTATION ≪≪ *Ezra Pound*

O Generation of the thoroughly smug
        and thoroughly uncomfortable,
I have seen fishermen picnicking in the sun,
I have seen them with untidy families,
I have seen their smiles full of teeth
        and heard ungainly laughter.
And I am happier than you are,
And they were happier than I am;
And the fish swim in the lake
        and do not even own clothing.

LEISURE ≪≪ *W. H. Davies*

What is this life if, full of care,
We have no time to stand and stare.

No time to stand beneath the boughs
And stare as long as sheep or cows.

No time to see, when woods we pass,
Where squirrels hide their nuts in grass.

No time to see, in broad daylight,
Streams full of stars like skies at night.

No time to turn at Beauty's glance,
And watch her feet, how they can dance.

No time to wait till her mouth can
Enrich that smile her eyes began.

A poor life this if, full of care,
We have no time to stand and stare.

LOVE WALKED ALONE ⋘ *Stephen Crane*

Love walked alone.
The rocks cut her tender feet,
And the brambles tore her fair limbs.
There came a companion to her,
But, alas, he was no help,
For his name was heart's pain.

PROVIDE, PROVIDE ⋘ *Robert Frost*

The witch that came (the withered hag)
To wash the steps with pail and rag,
Was once the beauty Abishag,

The picture pride of Hollywood.
Too many fall from great and good
For you to doubt the likelihood.

Die early and avoid the fate.
Or if predestined to die late,
Make up your mind to die in state.

Make the whole stock exchange your own!
If need be occupy a throne,
Where nobody can call *you* crone.

Some have relied on what they knew;
Others on being simply true.
What worked for them might work for you.

No memory of having starred
Atones for later disregard,
Or keeps the end from being hard.

Better to go down dignified
With boughten friendship at your side
Than none at all. Provide, provide!

THE EXPENSE OF SPIRIT IN A WASTE OF SHAME ⟨⟨⟨ *William Shakespeare*

The expense of spirit in a waste of shame
Is lust in action, and till action, lust
Is perjured, murd'rous, bloody, full of blame,
Savage, extreme, rude, cruel, not to trust,
Enjoyed no sooner but despisèd straight,
Past reason hunted, and no sooner had,
Past reason hated, as a swallowed bait,
On purpose laid to make the taker mad.
Mad in pursuit and in possession so,
Had, having, and in quest to have, extreme,
A bliss in proof, and proved, a very woe.
Before, a joy proposed, behind a dream.
　　All this the world well knows, yet none knows well
　　To shun the heaven that leads men to this hell.

10 ⋘ learn how to judge

Having learned some of the skills for surmounting the obstacles to understanding and for making that understanding secure, you are now ready to engage in the last and highest art of intelligent reading, namely, the art of making reasoned critical judgments. This art is last, for only the fool judges before he understands; and it is the highest, for it leads to the highest pleasure for the reader—the appreciation of genuine excellence.

But before entering into the problem of judging we ought first to come to terms with the common view that denies the possibility of objective critical judgments in artistic matters. According to this argument, everything in the fine arts is a matter of taste and opinion and consequently one is free to like what he likes when he likes it without fear of contradiction. We must admit at once that there is a grain of truth in this relativistic view. For one thing, it is easily verified that persons may have opposing opinions about the same poem. This may be because they are evaluating different aspects of the work, or because they are evaluating the same aspect but according to different standards of judgment. For example, one critic may be concerned solely with the quality of style, another may judge in terms of the complexity and scope of thought employed, yet another may judge in terms of the variety and depth of characterization, or yet another may attempt to estimate whether the poem is likely to have a good or bad influence upon people's thoughts and behavior in terms of social, moral, political, and religious values. Or they may be concerned with the quality of style, for example, and yet disagree as to what constitutes excellence of style. And so on.

Insofar as there are a variety of things to evaluate and different standards by which one may do so, and insofar as the critic is free to choose any one of them at a given time in the light of his interests and taste, the relativists are right. It does not follow, however, that there can be no objective judgments. Once a given aspect of the work is in question and a standard of value is selected, the critic may objectively argue that one work is better than another, for it is possible to compare poems in terms of how well they live up to the chosen standard. Just as we learn that a high jump of seven feet is extraordinary by comparing it with past performances, so too we judge the excellence, say, of a given character portrayal in the light of the performances of recognized masters of the art such as Dickens or Tolstoi.

The first important decision, then, in making a critical judgment is to determine what aspect of the work you want to evaluate and what standards to apply. There is no reason why full-scale criticism ought not to invoke the whole range of evaluative questions, extending from matters of diction to the social and moral consequences of literary works. Indeed, you should take every opportunity in your reading to develop principles that will allow you to recognize distinguished use of language, to assess the novelty and soundness of thought, to discern the skills that produce a vivid rendition of the dramatic scene, to savor the qualities of the artist's particular sensibility and view of life, and to judge the poet's views against the background of his time. Such principles (some of them are suggested in the Appendix) will surely widen your mind and provide grounds for more intelligent critical judgments.

However, without in any way denying the importance of these general standards of judgment, we wish in this chapter to concentrate upon a principle of evaluation that may profitably be applied when a poem is considered—as it has been considered throughout this book—as an adaptation of poetic means to a particular artistic end. That is to say, we wish to locate the artistic excellence of a poem—how well the parts relate to the whole—and we have a particular conception of poetic form, as explained in the preceding chapters, which will enable us to derive a standard for evaluating the organization of a given work. Since our theory of form postulates a hierarchical order of determination whereby the end gives shape to the context, the context so shaped controls the poet's choice of technical devices, and all these things determine for him his use of language, our standard is that all the parts should contribute to the intended effect, that everything which is needed is there, and that everything which is not needed has been excluded. We are, in effect, asking the question: from among the alternatives at his disposal, has the poet consistently made those choices which best achieve his end? Now the judgments which may follow from this principle are relative, as we have said, insofar as they depend upon locating some particular aspect of the poem to evaluate, and upon choosing a certain standard on the basis of which to do so. But once this has been done, such judgments may be argued objectively.

Our test question is, of course, more easily asked than answered, for in order to answer it you must re-think the poem in terms of its artistic purpose even as the poet had to re-think his poem as he wrote and revised it. And this may be done according to the topics developed so far in this book. Has the context been so organized as best to achieve the intended effect? Is the nature of the experience clear to the reader? Has the right kind of character been chosen? Is his state of mind appropriate? Have the techniques been so handled as best to present that context for the sake of that effect? Is the point of view the best for the given purpose? Have the materials been effectively selected and scaled? Has the most effective order

of disclosure and development been chosen? Has the language
been so managed as best to embody that context for the sake
of that end and being presented in such and such a way? And
so on. If there seem to be no alternatives that would improve
the choice at any point, then there is nothing to criticize. Or,
conversely, some of the choices, when measured against the alternatives, may seem clumsy and ill-judged. The requirements
of the form have either been met or they have not.

But these are merely minimal requirements, for they direct
us to inquire simply whether everything fits. A second and
correlative principle would ask not just whether all the parts
relate effectively to the whole but also whether they do so in
the *most* effective way imaginable. Has the poet made the most
out of his poetic problem? Has he not merely solved it but
done so in such a way as to surprise us by his powers and re-
sourcefulness? Has he exceeded what we have come to expect
from our reading of other poets writing similar poems? Has
he managed to strike off happy touches which we could not
have asked of him beforehand but which we must applaud after
we have seen them? Has he, in other words, managed to exploit
his materials by bringing out and developing all their potential
values, or has he simply been content to work them into a
completed whole and let it go at that?

Such are the uneasy but rewarding rites of formal criticism.
They call for the discipline of careful reading in order to re-
capture the organizing conception of the poem, for the imagination to conceive of alternative possibilities, and for the experience of a wide-ranging reader in order to permit the
comparisons necessary for the critical judgments of better and
worse. When we thus launch upon the great skills required for
literary criticism the shade of Master Pugliano hovers at our
back. Let us, then, avoid rhetoric and put the matter simply.
You must not expect to become a sound critic overnight, even

if you spend the whole time reading and re-reading this chapter.
But you can begin your apprenticeship right now by practicing
careful reading, imaginative reconstruction, and continued ex-
ploration of the realms of poetry.

In order to illustrate some of the problems of critical judgment, let us make a final visit to "Desert Places." We have
already shown how we think its reflective experience is unified
and how it is shaped to bring out in the reader feelings of
sympathy and pity. We have shown how its various devices of
manner work toward that end, and how the language plays its
part. Formally, it all seems of a piece: omitting or changing
or subtracting anything would spoil it. The first stanza is
needed in order to set the scene which serves as the basis for
the speaker's thoughts; the second is necessary in order to show
the reader the speaker's spiritual vacancy, for without it the
last stanza would make very little sense; the third stanza is
needed in order to show that the speaker sees that vacancy as
reflected in the scene, and again this is required in order for the
last stanza to mean anything; and the last stanza, as the culmi-
nation and conclusion of all that has gone before, is clearly
indispensable. All of this is needed if the reader is to feel the
proper sympathetic shudder. Having this experience, furthermore, placed before the reader in any point of view other than
the protagonist's present point of view would tend to diminish the immediacy and vividness required to stimulate sympathy
in the reader. Beginning sooner, or later; ending sooner, or later;
or leaving any elements out would tend to diminish the intelligi-
bility and force of the experience. Expanding certain parts or
contracting them would tend to misplace the proportions and
emphases needed. Changing the order from the chronological
to some other sequence would tend to cloud the development
of the reflection and the force of its conclusion. And heightening

or depressing the style would tend to give the reader a distorted picture of the experience.

We may say, then, that the poem has achieved the minimum condition of formal excellence—all of the parts are related to a single end. But our criticism can go further than that. Not only did Frost know what was needed for his poem, but he also knew how to make the most of its potentialities. The experience of the poem, as we have seen, involves a movement of the speaker's attention from the desolation of the wintry scene to his own internal spiritual barrenness. A lesser poet might well have made this transition in the second stanza: "And I too am a winter field. . . ." Frost, however, solved the problem more brilliantly. After the immediate scene is established, he sends his speaker's thoughts not inward but in widening circles; in the third stanza they leap ahead in time and, in the first part of the fourth, they leap outward into space. From the "empty spaces between stars" at the furthest fringe of human imagination, attention is suddenly reversed to the innermost being of the speaker, where unexpectedly and yet most plausibly the greatest desolation is to be found.

A second special virtue of the poem is to be found in Frost's way of desolating his scene, whose ominous quality is induced by the vision of a powerful, meaningless, indifferent nature pressing upon man and his works. The field, an instance of man's effort to impose order upon nature, is swiftly going under—"a few weeds and stubble showing last." The untamed woods are taking it back. Even the animals are "smothered" in their lairs. Not only does this vision of an encroaching blankness desolate the immediate scene, but it also gives a special poignancy to the final lines of the poem. If man is seen as the only counterforce to the mindless encroachments of nature, how much more terrifying, then, is the speaker's awareness that the enemy is already within his own private gates.

The perfect poem is rarely written, and consequently the critical reader must learn to handle defects as well as virtues. For example, in this poem, we might well be disturbed by Frost's manner of portraying the final recognition of internal despair. He loses control of his normally suggestive and subdued colloquial style in the last stanza and introduces inadvertently a note of flippancy quite inappropriate to the occasion. In the first place, the word "scare" seems scarcely adequate to the emotion that the speaker must be feeling at this moment. Moreover, it is difficult to avoid reading the last four lines as an unseemly boast ("if you want to hear about troubles, just listen to my story"). The inadequacy of diction and tone thus confuses the reader's response to the poem at the most critical point.

These remarks should suggest to you what is involved in the question of formal excellence. Let us remind you once more that there are many other standards for judging a poem or a poet. We merely urge that the formal method that we have advanced in this chapter is one that brings you into closest contact with the poet as a maker of poems. We trust that you have glimpsed some of the excitement that can arise from this strenuous form of critical exercise and that you will now want to continue your poetic education on your own.

appendix ⋘ a look beyond

Throughout this book our central concern has been to provide the critical questions that will lead you to an understanding of individual poems. After all, for the poet, the solution of the artistic problems of a particular poem is what occupies his attention at any given moment in his writing career, and, for the reader, enjoyment comes not from poetry in general but from reading particular poems. However, once you have come to terms with the internal organization of a poem and have made some effort to assess the choices of the poet in the light of that organization, there remains yet a further dimension to reading that can increase your powers of discrimination and add to your enjoyment, namely, the dimension that emerges when you view the poem in relation to other poems. It is only in the light of a wide range of poetic possibilities that you can begin to savor the unique quality of a poem, to appreciate what is original and what is commonplace in it, or to judge whether it represents an artistic victory or defeat.

There are, of course, many relationships in terms of which a poem may be viewed. To illustrate the problems that arise at this level of reading, we shall concentrate on three possible relationships: (1) that provided by the poet's other poems; (2) that provided by the poems of other poets of his own period; and (3) that provided by the poems of poets of other periods. In this kind of inquiry the governing problem is to determine in what ways a given poem resembles and in what ways it differs from the author's other poetic writings, or the poems of his period, or the poetry that came before and after. The relationships discovered may be seen as ever-broadening circles of reference. To carry out such a program of comparative reading the student obviously must sharpen his powers of generalization. He must consider how one may go about characterizing the poetic output of a single poet, or of a given period, or of a given country over a period of time. In what follows we shall suggest some methods for developing generalizations in these several areas of inquiry and point out some of the pitfalls that lie in the way.

I

When the distinctive qualities of a given poet are the object of inquiry, the first step, of course, is to take note of the recurring traits that appear throughout his poetry. Here the trick is to provide yourself with topics of comparison that will uncover significant similarities and differences. There are, alas, no rules for making relevant and interesting discoveries, but we offer the following topics in the hope that they might suggest to you fruitful generalizations.

One of the obvious clues to the special world of a poet is his way with words. As you read widely in the work of an author you begin to develop a sense of a characteristic quality of style. Inquiry at this level might well begin with an effort to define this quality. Is it more elevated than ordinary speech (as in the case of Milton)? Or is it fastidious and exotic (as in the case of Wallace Stevens), wittily urbane (as in the case of Auden), sensuously opulent (as in the case of Keats), plain and straightforward (as in the case of Edwin Muir), or casual and colloquial (as in the case of Robert Frost)? After you have settled on the precise quality that distinguishes the poet's style, you might then seek out the particular devices of language which combine to produce this quality. Does it lie in his choice of diction? Some poets, for example, have a favorite set of words that carry unusual weight with them (as in the case of Dylan Thomas, whose early poems generate a special flavor through their obsessive iteration of such words as "fork," "fellow," "vein," "worm," or "half"). Are the poet's words concrete or abstract, long or short, technical or everyday, strange or familiar, standard or regional?

You ought then to consider what is contributed by the poet's manner of putting words together. Does he use the normal order of words or does he invert them? Is he sparing or generous with modifiers? Does he prefer simple or complex sentences? Does he like to construct his sentences so that phrase balances phrase and clause answers clause? Does he withhold his meaning until the end of the sentence? After surveying the poet's syntax you might then consider his use of comparisons. Does he rely heavily upon similes and metaphors? If so, from what areas of experience do they derive? Does he make use of symbolism? Is he fond of allusions? Does the poet have marked preferences for certain meters and stanza forms? Does he like to work out intricate relations between the stanza structure and the evolution of thought and feeling in the poem, or is he more content with a flexible blank verse that stamps no definite mold on the turns of thought? Such questions as these do not exhaust the stylistic devices that may contribute to the distinctive quality of a poet's style, but they should suggest the directions your inquiry might take.

Another area in which a poet may reveal his characteristic bent is his choice of material. If he is primarily given to the representation of imagined characters undergoing moments of experience, you ought to consider what types of activities he prefers—states of feeling, internal processes of describing, reflecting, deliberating, and meditating, or speeches addressed to other persons in the imagined scene. What types of circumstances usually stimulate this activity—occurrences in nature (as often is the case with Frost), scenes from the city (as with Cummings), human relationships (as with Browning), personal problems of value and conduct (as often with Wordsworth)? What is the character and personality of the person usually engaged in the experience? Here, as in almost every area of creative choice, the possibilities are endless. The characters may range from grave and lofty to flippant and irreverent, from emotionally expansive to stoically restrained, from innocent to sophisticated, from exuberant to world-weary. Then, too, you will want to inquire what qualities of thought mark the characteristic speaker of the poems. Does he have distinctive views regarding the nature of man and the universe? The proper conduct of man? The values of experience?

If the poet prefers to present ideas directly, relevant topics for characterizing him would include such matters as the persistent themes he employs and the way he develops them.

A third topic of comparison might well be the emotional response that the poet characteristically seeks to evoke through his ordering of language and context. Does he shape and combine elements of action and language in such a way as to elicit a distinctive shading of admiration, pity, indignation, laughter, sympathy, or surprise? As you have already seen, it is no easy matter to define the precise nature of your emotional response to a lyric experience. It is difficult enough to pinpoint the emotions aroused by the larger actions of a play or novel; to catch the nuance of a fleeting mood or subtle reflection in a lyric calls for the utmost care. One of the values of reading a large number of poems by a single poet is that it will aid you in making such discriminations.

In Chapters 7 and 8 we took up a variety of choices the poet must make in finding effective ways of unfolding his context—the choice of point of view, selection of detail, ordering of parts, the scale with which the several parts are to be handled, among others. Here, too, we may trace the preferences and habits that characterize a particular poet. Some poets are fond of elaborating the circumstances which give rise to the lyric activity before presenting the activity itself. Others plunge immediately into the experience of feeling or thinking and withhold its causes until the end or leave them to be inferred. Some poets prefer to make the connections between one thought and another explicit and others leave them to be worked out by the reader. In expository poems the poet may have characteristic ways of elaborating his subject—amplification by details, by examples, or by comparison.

Using such topics as we have just suggested, you might proceed to draw up a formidable list of persistent artistic practices running through the work of a particular poet. Yet beyond mere list-making a further question beckons: is there some central poetic concern or some pervasive view of the world engaging the artist's attention over a period of time which explains his predilection for certain poetic contexts, certain lyric forms, certain techniques of representation, and certain devices of diction? This notion of a central poetic concern—what we have called the poet's vision—might be understood if we think of a poet as having a particular susceptibility to certain kinds of experience, or a preoccupation with certain moral or intellectual problems, or a reliance upon certain assumptions about life. These susceptibilities, preoccupations, or assumptions may operate at moments of inspiration in influencing the many choices that creative writing requires.

The poetic vein that seems to nourish much of Hopkins' poetry, for example, is his susceptibility to moments of intense religious feeling, a feeling that ranges from a fervent joy and wonder at manifestations in nature of "God's grandeur"—a kestrel riding the air, a kingfisher in a flashing dive, or a fresh spring day—to agonizing despair when he feels no longer sustained by God's grace. His interest in such manifestations is influenced by his theological assumption that each thing has its own peculiar essence ("inscape") and that when that essence is expressed in the proper functioning of the object or living being, God's glory is most fully revealed. But whether he feels in or out of a state of grace, Hopkins tends to write lyrics portraying intense moments of passion. Consequently his poems begin at a fever pitch, elaborate a single burst of thought or feeling, and are soon done (the sonnet provides his favorite stanza pattern). His utterances are exclamatory, marked by the strong but irregular rhythms of passionate speech, and intensified by heavy alliteration, internal rhyme, and onomatopoeic effects. And most characteristic of all, his impatient urgency causes him to jam nouns together without the connectives that normally accompany deliberate speech.

It takes patience, devoted reading, and many a tentative speculation to sift the works of a poet for his characteristic vein and to perceive the connections between his susceptibilities, preoccupations, assumptions, and his persistent poetic practices. Unity, however, should not be enforced for its own sake. It is always important to remember that a poet may have more than one poetic vein, that he may work in a variety of modes. Indeed, it is useful to distinguish between poets who have but one voice and those who have many. It is also important to remember that a poet may undergo development during his artistic career. William Butler Yeats, for example, began as a romantic poet aiming at nebulous and tenuous effects, but in mid career he began to sense the powers of plainness and directness in poetry. Thus, in seeking the poet's vision, you will do well to keep in mind the possibility of diversity.

It may have occurred to you by now that the effort to define a poet's vision can be an interesting inquiry in its own right. To grow familiar with the particular quality of an artist's imagination, to observe the range of his interests, and to trace out how his imagination and interests are bodied forth in his art are all ways of increasing your awareness of human possibilities. But more importantly, an understanding of the poet's vision allows you to return to his poems as a better reader and critic. Having learned to recognize his special habits of language, his favorite contexts, and his preferred techniques for disclosing his subject, you will be that much more adept at coming to artistic terms with any one of his poems; and, having surveyed the range of his work, you will be that much more able to see how that poem was, perhaps, a tentative experiment, or that it achieved a triumphant solution to a persistent problem, or that it merely repeated earlier efforts, or that it marked a turning point in his career.

II

The second relationship that we suggested takes you beyond the poems of a single poet to the body of poetry produced by his contemporaries. A consideration of the poetic conventions that influenced the writing of many poets in a given time and place is a necessary corrective to your initial estimate of an individual poet, for without it you may mistakenly assign to personal vision what in reality belongs to the age. As you widen your reading of the poetry of a period, you will become aware of a variety of conventions.

In some periods, the diction that is felt suitable to poetry of various kinds is strongly fixed; whereas at other times, the poet is free to experiment in a wide range of styles. In some periods, metaphor and symbol may be the height of fashion; in others, poetic distinction may be sought in the rhetorical figures of balance, parallelism, or antithesis.

Periods may also be characterized by the popularity of certain poetic forms. For example, during the eighteenth century in England rhetorical poetry, which aimed at either praise or ridicule, was much in vogue, whereas in the early nineteenth century lyrics of emotion and meditation became more prominent.

You will also find conventions of thought and attitude permeating the poetry of a given time and place. Elizabethan love poetry, for example, draws heavily upon the tradition of courtly love, a complex of conventions stemming from the late Middle Ages which prescribed the proper emotions between the high-born lady and her devoted knight, the duties of each, the language appropriate to their discourse. In the eighteenth century the concept of the Great Chain of Being provided an important framework for the discursive poetry of the period. In the twentieth century, to cite one final example, the mythology of Greece and of more primitive cultures became fashionable in literary art under the influence of such men as Frazer and Jung, who theorized that myths embody the fundamental patterns of human existence. As you can see, the topics for guiding an inquiry into the conventions of a period are similar to those we recommended for examining the poems of an individual poet—diction, techniques of representation, poetic forms, vision.

After establishing the various conventions that characterize a period you may ask whether it is possible to go on, as we did in the case of the poet's vision, to work out a synthesis for the age. One school of historians would say yes, but we would urge the utmost caution in such an endeavor. It is true that the poets of a given period may reveal a preoccupation with a common problem (for example, the conflict of religion and science, or the role of the poet in a materialistic society, or the problem of personal identity), but it is not likely that they all conceive of the problem in the same terms or that they find the same solutions in the same way. The diversity of temperaments, of values, and of views of life that we see around us in our own time should recommend to us a skeptical attitude toward such popular unifying rubrics as the Age of Reason, the Age of Romanticism, or the Age of Anxiety.

But it goes without saying that a widening knowledge of the poetic conventions of a period adds greatly to your ability to deal with the qualities of a single author and, even more importantly, with his individual poems. It will help you determine how far a given poem is dependent on conventions—whether the poem merely imitates conventions, whether it turns them to new artistic uses, or whether it ignores them altogether. Moreover, it will sometimes help explain those choices of the poet which do seem not to be specifically determined by his artistic purpose. There is nothing in the art of writing a love poem, for example, which demands that it be in a sonnet pattern; thus to understand Shakespeare's choice of the pattern in his cycle of love poems, we must look to the sonnet vogue in Elizabethan England.

III

The third relationship to which we called your attention adds the dimension of time. Here the aim is to acquire a sense of the changing characteristics of the poetic art from period to period. To trace the intricate lines of development in the lyric and to uncover the causes of change are undoubtedly the tasks of mature scholarship, but even the amateur may add zest to his reading by beginning his own list of observations regarding the evolution of conventions. One of the interesting experiments that may be carried out while you are reading through a poetry anthology is to take as a constant one of the topics we have discussed above and then ask what changes take place in that area from age to age. For example, you may take a certain poetic form—say, the serious meditative or deliberative lyric which concludes with an important solution or choice for the speaker (perhaps Milton's "Lycidas," Gray's "Elegy Written in a Country Churchyard," Keats' "Ode on a Grecian Urn," Arnold's "Dover Beach," and Yeats' "Sailing to Byzantium"). Then you might note what changes occur from period to period in the diction employed with the form, the types of situations that provoke the response, the premises that are involved in the solution or choice, the types of characters engaged in the experience, the nature of the conclusion, the devices of representation employed, and so on. Or you may hold a certain subject-matter constant (say, love, death, war, childhood, nature, or feminine beauty) and consider what variations it undergoes over a period of time. In what poetic forms does it appear? What images are associated with it? Is it treated lightly or seriously? Or you may hold a certain convention constant, such as the convention of the pastoral poem or the ode, and observe the variations it undergoes from generation to generation. Or you may trace the changes in poetic diction over a period of time, as Josephine Miles has done in her detailed studies of poetic language. Experiments of this kind are limited only by your curiosity and ingenuity, but they should all be aimed at refining your sense of what characterizes each age and at locating the sequence by which changes came about.

These, then, are some of the broad and far-reaching avenues that lead out from the study of single poems. To grow intimate with the ways of an individual poet, to savor his distinctive qualities in the setting of his own time, to glimpse the pattern of development of the poetic art of a given culture—these are all pleasurable exercises of the mind in their own right, but it should be remembered that their greatest value is that they bring you back to the individual poem with strengthened powers of discrimination and enjoyment. As we remarked earlier, poetry takes body and shape and comes alive only in the particular poem on the page before us.

﹡﹡ supplementary poems

The following poems have been arranged for further study and discussion according to the distinctions and suggestions made in the Appendix. They fall, therefore, into three groups: poems of a single poet, poems of the same period, and poems arranged chronologically through different periods. Each group, then, is designed to bring out certain aspects of poetic study and to raise certain questions appropriate thereto.

These patterns, however, are only a convenience for those who want to use them. The same poems may be used in any other way the instructor deems suitable, if only to add to the number of poems already appended to each of the seven working chapters.

I poems of a single poet: john keats ⫷⫷⫷

The following ten poems by John Keats provide an opportunity to assess the distinctive qualities that make up what we have called "a poet's vision." The problem here is to see if you can discover and formulate the special flavor of a Keatsian poem. To carry out this inquiry, we suggest that you ask of these poems the questions posed in section I of the Appendix. What are Keats's favorite words? What types of sentences does he use? What are his favorite sources of comparison? What types of circumstances serve to stimulate Keats's imagination? What ideas does he hold? What qualities of feeling? What poetic forms does he favor? What techniques of manner does he characteristically employ? What effects does he strive for? Which poems seem to be more successful in employing these characteristics? How wide is his range of poetic forms? Do you find some central poetic concern or some pervasive view of the world which might explain Keats's predilection for certain poetic contexts, certain lyric forms, certain techniques of representation, and certain types of diction?

We have included some important letters by Keats which help to shed light on these problems.

It may be useful to know a few salient features of his biography. Keats was born in 1795, the son of the head ostler at a London livery stable. Orphaned by the age of fourteen, he was apprenticed by his practical-minded guardian to a surgeon and was qualified to practice as an apothecary by the age of twenty-one. Under the influence of literary friends, among whom were some of England's leading Romantic writers, he soon gave himself over entirely to the writing of poetry. From that point on, Keats developed his poetic talent with astonishing speed, following the call of that talent independently of the strong poetic influences around him.

In the year 1818, when Keats was twenty-three, the circumstances of his life began to darken. His brother George had emigrated to Kentucky and was in financial distress, his younger brother Tom died of tuberculosis, and Keats himself had the first omens of the tuberculosis that was to end his life three years later. Moreover, in the late fall of 1818 he fell desperately in love with Fanny Brawne. Although they became engaged, Keats's poverty and illness made marriage unthinkable.

In 1820 Keats sought the milder climate of Italy; he died in Rome on February 23, 1821.

ON THE SEA ⋘

It keeps eternal whisperings around
  Desolate shores, and with its mighty swell
  Gluts twice ten thousand Caverns, till the spell
Of Hecate leaves them their old shadowy sound.
Often 'tis in such gentle temper found,
  That scarcely will the very smallest shell
  Be mov'd for days from where it sometime fell,
When last the winds of Heaven were unbound.
Oh ye! who have your eye-balls vex'd and tir'd,
  Feast them upon the wideness of the Sea;
    Oh ye! whose ears are dinn'd with uproar rude,
  Or fed too much with cloying melody—
    Sit ye near some old Cavern's Mouth, and brood
Until ye start, as if the sea-nymphs quir'd!
[*1817*]

ON SEEING THE ELGIN MARBLES
FOR THE FIRST TIME ⋘

My spirit is too weak; mortality
  Weighs heavily on me like unwilling sleep,
  And each imagin'd pinnacle and steep
Of godlike hardship tells me I must die
Like a sick eagle looking at the sky.
  Yet 'tis a gentle luxury to weep
  That I have not the cloudy winds to keep
Fresh for the opening of the morning's eye.
Such dim-conceived glories of the brain
  Bring round the heart an indescribable feud;

So do these wonders a most dizzy pain,
   That mingles Grecian grandeur with the rude
Wasting of old Time—with a billowy main,
   A sun, a shadow of a magnitude.
[*1817*]

From SLEEP AND POETRY ⟪

(LINES 53–162; 270–312)

O Poesy! for thee I grasp my pen
That am not yet a glorious denizen
Of thy wide heaven; yet, to my ardent prayer,
Yield from thy sanctuary some clear air,
Smoothed for intoxication by the breath
Of flowering bays, that I may die a death
Of luxury, and my young spirit follow
The morning sun-beams to the great Apollo
Like a fresh sacrifice; or, if I can bear
The o'erwhelming sweets, 'twill bring to me the fair
Visions of all places: a bowery nook
Will be elysium—an eternal book
Whence I may copy many a lovely saying
About the leaves, and flowers—about the playing
Of nymphs in woods, and fountains; and the shade
Keeping a silence round a sleeping maid;
And many a verse from so strange influence
That we must ever wonder how, and whence
It came. Also imaginings will hover
Round my fire-side, and haply there discover
Vistas of solemn beauty, where I'd wander
In happy silence, like the clear Meander
Through its lone vales; and where I found a spot

Of awfuller shade, or an enchanted grot,
Or a green hill o'erspread with chequered dress
Of flowers, and fearful from its loveliness,
Write on my tablets all that was permitted,
All that was for our human senses fitted.
Then the events of this wide world I'd seize
Like a strong giant, and my spirit teaze
Till at its shoulders it should proudly see
Wings to find out an immortality.

Stop and consider! life is but a day;
A fragile dew-drop on its perilous way
From a tree's summit; a poor Indian's sleep
While his boat hastens to the monstrous steep
Of Montmorenci. Why so sad a moan?
Life is the rose's hope while yet unblown;
The reading of an ever-changing tale;
The light uplifting of a maiden's veil;
A pigeon tumbling in clear summer air;
A laughing school-boy, without grief or care,
Riding the springy branches of an elm.

O for ten years, that I may overwhelm
Myself in poesy; so I may do the deed
That my own soul has to itself decreed.
Then will I pass the countries that I see
In long perspective, and continually
Taste their pure fountains. First the realm I'll pass
Of Flora, and old Pan: sleep in the grass,
Feed upon apples red, and strawberries,
And choose each pleasure that my fancy sees;
Catch the white-handed nymphs in shady places,
To woo sweet kisses from averted faces,—
Play with their fingers, touch their shoulders white

Into a pretty shrinking with a bite
As hard as lips can make it: till agreed,
A lovely tale of human life we'll read.
And one will teach a tame dove how it best
May fan the cool air gently o'er my rest;
Another, bending o'er her nimble tread,
Will set a green robe floating round her head,
And still will dance with ever varied ease,
Smiling upon the flowers and the trees:
Another will entice me on, and on
Through almond blossoms and rich cinnamon;
Till in the bosom of a leafy world
We rest in silence, like two gems upcurl'd
In the recesses of a pearly shell.

And can I ever bid these joys farewell?
Yes, I must pass them for a nobler life,
Where I may find the agonies, the strife
Of human hearts: for lo! I see afar,
O'ersailing the blue cragginess, a car
And steeds with streamy manes—the charioteer
Looks out upon the winds with glorious fear:
And now the numerous tramplings quiver lightly
Along a huge cloud's ridge; and now with sprightly
Wheel downward come they into fresher skies,
Tipt round with silver from the sun's bright eyes.
Still downward with capacious whirl they glide;
And now I see them on the green-hill's side
In breezy rest among the nodding stalks.
The charioteer with wond'rous gesture talks
To the trees and mountains; and there soon appear
Shapes of delight, of mystery, and fear,
Passing along before a dusky space
Made by some mighty oaks: as they would chase

Some ever-fleeting music on they sweep.
Lo! how they murmur, laugh, and smile, and weep:
Some with upholden hand and mouth severe;
Some with their faces muffled to the ear
Between their arms; some, clear in youthful bloom,
Go glad and smilingly athwart the gloom;
Some looking back, and some with upward gaze;
Yes, thousands in a thousand different ways
Flit onward—now a lovely wreath of girls
Dancing their sleek hair into tangled curls;
And now broad wings. Most awfully intent
The driver of those steeds is forward bent,
And seems to listen: O that I might know
All that he writes with such a hurrying glow.

The visions all are fled—the car is fled
Into the light of heaven, and in their stead
A sense of real things comes doubly strong,
And, like a muddy stream, would bear along
My soul to nothingness: but I will strive
Against all doubtings, and will keep alive
The thought of that same chariot, and the strange
Journey it went.
　　　　. . . . .
Will not some say that I presumptuously
Have spoken? that from hastening disgrace
'Twere better far to hide my foolish face?
That whining boyhood should with reverence bow
Ere the dread thunderbolt could reach? How!
If I do hide myself, it sure shall be
In the very fane, the light of Poesy:
If I do fall, at least I will be laid
Beneath the silence of a poplar shade;
And over me the grass shall be smooth shaven:

And there shall be a kind memorial graven.
But off Despondence! miserable bane!
They should not know thee, who athirst to gain
A noble end, are thirsty every hour.
What though I am not wealthy in the dower
Of spanning wisdom; though I do not know
The shiftings of the mighty winds that blow
Hither and thither all the changing thoughts
Of man: though no great minist'ring reason sorts
Out the dark mysteries of human souls
To clear conceiving: yet there ever rolls
A vast idea before me, and I glean
Therefrom my liberty; thence too I've seen
The end and aim of Poesy. 'Tis clear
As anything most true; as that the year
Is made of the four seasons—manifest
As a large cross, some old cathedral's crest,
Lifted to the white clouds. Therefore should I
Be but the essence of deformity,
A coward, did my very eye-lids wink
At speaking out what I have dared to think.
Ah! rather let me like a madman run
Over some precipice; let the hot sun
Melt my Dedalian wings, and drive me down
Convuls'd and headlong! Stay! an inward frown
Of conscience bids me be more calm awhile.
An ocean dim, sprinkled with many an isle,
Spreads awfully before me. How much toil!
How many days! what desperate turmoil!
Ere I can have explored its widenesses.
Ah, what a task! upon my bended knees,
I could unsay those—no, impossible!
Impossible!

[*Nov. Dec. 1816*]

WHEN I HAVE FEARS ⫷

When I have fears that I may cease to be
    Before my pen has glean'd my teeming brain,
Before high-piled books, in charact'ry,
    Hold like rich garners the full-ripen'd grain;
When I behold, upon the night's starr'd face,
    Huge cloudy symbols of a high romance,
And think that I may never live to trace
    Their shadows, with the magic hand of chance;
And when I feel, fair creature of an hour,
    That I shall never look upon thee more,
Never have relish in the faery power
    Of unreflecting love!—then on the shore
Of the wide world I stand alone, and think
Till Love and Fame to nothingness do sink.
[*1818*]

LA BELLE DAME SANS MERCI ⫷

O what can ail thee, Knight at arms,
    Alone and palely loitering?
The sedge has withered from the Lake,
    And no birds sing!

O what can ail thee, Knight at arms,
    So haggard, and so woe begone?
The Squirrel's granary is full
    And the harvest's done.

I see a lily on thy brow
  With anguish moist and fever dew,
And on thy cheeks a fading rose
  Fast withereth too—

I met a Lady in the Meads,
  Full beautiful, a faery's child,
Her hair was long, her foot was light
  And her eyes were wild—

I made a Garland for her head,
  And bracelets too, and fragrant Zone
She look'd at me as she did love
  And made sweet moan—

I set her on my pacing steed
  And nothing else saw all day long
For sidelong would she bend and sing
  A faery's song—

She found me roots of relish sweet
  And honey wild and manna dew
And sure in language strange she said
  I love thee true—

She took me to her elfin grot
  And there she wept and sighed full sore,
And there I shut her wild wild eyes
  With kisses four.

And there she lulled me asleep
  And there I dream'd, Ah Woe betide!
The latest dream I ever dreamt
  On the cold hill side.

I saw pale Kings, and Princes too
   Pale warriors, death pale were they all;
Who cried, La belle dame sans merci
   Thee hath in thrall.

I saw their starv'd lips in the gloam
   With horrid warning gaped wide,
And I awoke, and found me here
   On the cold hill's side.

And this is why I sojourn here
   Alone and palely loitering;
Though the sedge is withered from the Lake,
   And no birds sing—
[*1819*]

TO AUTUMN ≪

I

Season of mists and mellow fruitfulness,
   Close bosom-friend of the maturing sun;
Conspiring with him how to load and bless
   With fruit the vines that round the thatch-eves run;
To bend with apples the moss'd cottage-trees,
   And fill all fruit with ripeness to the core;
     To swell the gourd, and plump the hazel shells
   With a sweet kernel; to set budding more,
And still more, later flowers for the bees,
Until they think warm days will never cease,
   For Summer has o'er-brimm'd their clammy cells.

II

Who hath not seen thee oft amid thy store?
  Sometimes whoever seeks abroad may find
Thee sitting careless on a granary floor,
  Thy hair soft-lifted by the winnowing wind;
Or on a half-reap'd furrow sound asleep,
    Drows'd with the fume of poppies, while thy hook
      Spares the next swath and all its twined flowers:
And sometimes like a gleaner thou dost keep
    Steady thy laden head across a brook;
    Or by a cyder-press, with patient look,
      Thou watchest the last oozings hours by hours.

III

Where are the songs of Spring? Ay, where are they?
  Think not of them, thou hast thy music too,—
While barred clouds bloom the soft-dying day,
  And touch the stubble-plains with rosy hue;
Then in a wailful choir the small gnats mourn
    Among the river sallows, borne aloft
      Or sinking as the light wind lives or dies;
And full-grown lambs loud bleat from hilly bourn;
    Hedge-crickets sing; and now with treble soft
    The red-breast whistles from a garden-croft;
      And gathering swallows twitter in the skies.
[*1819*]

ODE ON MELANCHOLY ⋘

I

No, no, go not to Lethe, neither twist
  Wolf's-bane, tight-rooted, for its poisonous wine;
Nor suffer thy pale forehead to be kiss'd
  By nightshade, ruby grape of Proserpine;

Make not your rosary of yew-berries,
  Nor let the beetle, nor the death-moth be
    Your mournful Psyche, nor the downy owl
A partner in your sorrow's mysteries:
  For shade to shade will come too drowsily,
    And drown the wakeful anguish of the soul.

II

But when the melancholy fit shall fall
  Sudden from heaven like a weeping cloud,
That fosters the droop-headed flowers all,
  And hides the green hill in an April shroud;
Then glut thy sorrow on a morning rose,
  Or on the rainbow of the salt sand-wave,
    Or on the wealth of globed peonies;
Or if thy mistress some rich anger shows,
  Emprison her soft hand, and let her rave,
    And feed deep, deep upon her peerless eyes.

III

She dwells with Beauty—Beauty that must die;
  And Joy, whose hand is ever at his lips
Bidding adieu; and aching Pleasure nigh,
  Turning to Poison while the bee-mouth sips:
Ay, in the very temple of Delight
  Veil'd Melancholy has her sovran shrine,
    Though seen of none save him whose strenuous tongue
  Can burst Joy's grape against his palate fine;
His soul shall taste the sadness of her might,
    And be among her cloudy trophies hung.
[*1819*]

ODE TO A NIGHTINGALE ⟪⟪⟪

I

My heart aches, and a drowsy numbness pains
　　My sense, as though of hemlock I had drunk,
Or emptied some dull opiate to the drains
　　One minute past, and Lethe-wards had sunk:
'Tis not through envy of thy happy lot,
　　But being too happy in thine happiness,—
　　　　That thou, light-winged Dryad of the trees,
　　　　　　In some melodious plot
　　Of beechen green, and shadows numberless,
　　　　Singest of summer in full-throated ease.

II

O, for a draught of vintage! that hath been
　　Cool'd a long age in the deep-delved earth,
Tasting of Flora and the country green,
　　Dance, and Provençal song, and sunburnt mirth!
O for a beaker full of the warm South,
　　Full of the true, the blushful Hippocrene,
　　　　With beaded bubbles winking at the brim,
　　　　　　And purple-stained mouth;
　　That I might drink, and leave the world unseen,
　　　　And with thee fade away into the forest dim:

III

Fade far away, dissolve, and quite forget
　　What thou among the leaves hast never known,
The weariness, the fever, and the fret
　　Here, where men sit and hear each other groan;

Where palsy shakes a few, sad, last gray hairs,
　　Where youth grows pale, and spectre-thin, and dies;
　　　Where but to think is to be full of sorrow
　　　　And leaden-eyed despairs,
　　　Where Beauty cannot keep her lustrous eyes,
　　　　Or new Love pine at them beyond to-morrow.

IV

Away! away! for I will fly to thee,
　　Not charioted by Bacchus and his pards,
But on the viewless wings of Poesy,
　　Though the dull brain perplexes and retards:
Already with thee! tender is the night,
　　And haply the Queen-Moon is on her throne,
　　　Cluster'd around by all her starry Fays;
　　　　But here there is no light,
　　Save what from heaven is with the breezes blown
　　　Through verdurous glooms and winding mossy ways.

V

I cannot see what flowers are at my feet,
　　Nor what soft incense hangs upon the boughs,
But, in embalmed darkness, guess each sweet
　　Wherewith the seasonable month endows
The grass, the thicket, and the fruit-tree wild;
　　White hawthorn, and the pastoral eglantine;
　　　Fast fading violets cover'd up in leaves;
　　　　And mid-May's eldest child,
　　The coming musk-rose, full of dewy wine,
　　　The murmurous haunt of flies on summer eves.

VI

Darkling I listen; and, for many a time
　　I have been half in love with easeful Death,

Call'd him soft names in many a mused rhyme,
　To take into the air my quiet breath;
Now more than ever seems it rich to die,
　To cease upon the midnight with no pain,
　　While thou art pouring forth thy soul abroad
　　　In such an ecstasy!
　Still wouldst thou sing, and I have ears in vain—
　　To thy high requiem become a sod.

VII

Thou wast not born for death, immortal Bird!
　No hungry generations tread thee down;
The voice I hear this passing night was heard
　In ancient days by emperor and clown:
　Perhaps the self-same song that found a path
　　Through the sad heart of Ruth, when, sick for home,
　　　She stood in tears amid the alien corn;
　　　　The same that oft-times hath
　Charm'd magic casements, opening on the foam
　　Of perilous seas, in faery lands forlorn.

VIII

Forlorn! the very word is like a bell
　To toll me back from thee to my sole self!
Adieu! the fancy cannot cheat so well
　　As she is fam'd to do, deceiving elf.
Adieu! adieu! thy plaintive anthem fades
　Past the near meadows, over the still stream,
　　Up the hill-side; and now 'tis buried deep
　　　In the next valley-glades:
　Was it a vision, or a waking dream?
　　Fled is that music:—Do I wake or sleep?
[*1819*]

BRIGHT STAR, WOULD I WERE STEDFAST
AS THOU ART— ≪

[Written on a blank page in Shakespeare's Poems,
facing *A Lover's Complaint.*]

Bright star, would I were stedfast as thou art—
   Not in lone splendour hung aloft the night
And watching, with eternal lids apart,
   Like nature's patient, sleepless Eremite,
The moving waters at their priestlike task
   Of pure ablution round earth's human shores,
Or gazing on the new soft fallen mask
   Of snow upon the mountains and the moors—
No—yet still stedfast, still unchangeable,
   Pillow'd upon my fair love's ripening breast,
To feel for ever its soft fall and swell,
   Awake for ever in a sweet unrest,
Still, still to hear her tender-taken breath,
And so live ever—or else swoon to death.
   [*1819*]

TO FANNY ≪

I cry your mercy—pity—love!—aye, love!
   Merciful love that tantalizes not,
One-thoughted, never-wandering, guileless love,
   Unmask'd, and being seen—without a blot!
O! let me have thee whole,—all—all—be mine!
   That shape, that fairness, that sweet minor zest
Of love, your kiss,—those hands, those eyes divine,
   That warm, white, lucent, million-pleasured breast,—

Yourself—your soul—in pity give me all,
   Withhold no atom's atom or I die,
Or living on perhaps, your wretched thrall,
   Forget, in the mist of idle misery,
Life's purposes,—the palate of my mind
Losing its gust, and my ambition blind!
[*1819*]

LETTERS OF KEATS
To George and Thomas Keats

Hampstead, December 22, 1817

My Dear Brothers—I must crave your pardon for not
having written ere this. . . . I saw Kean return to the public in
Richard III., and finely he did it, and, at the request of
Reynolds, I went to criticise his *Duke* in Rich^d.—the critique
is in to-day's Champion, which I send you with the Examiner,
in which you will find very proper lamentation on the obsoletion
of Christmas Gambols and pastimes: but it was mixed up with
so much egotism of that drivelling nature that pleasure is
entirely lost. Hone the publisher's trial, you must find very
amusing, and as Englishmen very encouraging: his *Not Guilty*
is a thing, which not to have been, would have dulled still more
Liberty's Emblazoning—Lord Ellenborough has been paid in
his own coin—Wooler and Hone have done us an essential
service. I have had two very pleasant evenings with Dilke yesterday and to-day, and am at this moment just come from him,
and feel in the humour to go on with this, begun in the morning,
and from which he came to fetch me. I spent Friday evening
with Wells and went next morning to see *Death on the Pale
horse*. It is a wonderful picture, when West's age is considered;

but there is nothing to be intense upon, no women one feels mad to kiss, no face swelling into reality. The excellence of every art is its intensity, capable of making all disagreeables evaporate from their being in close relationship with Beauty and Truth—Examine King Lear, and you will find this exemplified throughout; but in this picture we have unpleasantness without any momentous depth of speculation excited, in which to bury its repulsiveness—The picture is larger than Christ rejected.

I dined with Haydon the Sunday after you left, and had a very pleasant day. I dined too (for I have been out too much lately) with Horace Smith and met his two Brothers with Hill and Kingston and one Du Bois, they only served to convince me how superior humour is to wit, in respect to enjoyment—These men say things which make one start, without making one feel; they are all alike; their manners are alike; they all know fashionables; they have all a mannerism in their very eating and drinking, in their mere handling a Decanter. They talked of Kean and his low company—would I were with that company instead of yours said I to myself! I know such like acquaintance will never do for me and yet I am going to Reynolds, on Wednesday. Brown and Dilke walked with me and back from the Christmas pantomime. I had not a dispute, but a disquisition, with Dilke upon various subjects; several things dove-tailed in my mind, and at once it struck me what quality went to form a Man of Achievement, especially in Literature, and which Shakespeare possessed so enormously—I mean *Negative Capability*, that is, when a man is capable of being in uncertainties, mysteries, doubts, without any irritable reaching after fact and reason. Coleridge, for instance, would let go by a fine isolated verisimilitude caught from the Penetralium of mystery, from being incapable of remaining content with half-knowledge. This pursued through volumes would perhaps take us no further than this, that with a great poet the sense of

Beauty overcomes every other consideration, or rather obliterates all consideration.

Shelley's poem is out and there are words about its being objected to, as much as Queen Mab was. Poor Shelley I think he has his Quota of good qualities, in sooth la! Write soon to your most sincere friend and affectionate Brother

JOHN.

To Richard Woodhouse

Hampstead, October 27, 1818

MY DEAR WOODHOUSE—Your letter gave me great satisfaction, more on account of its friendliness than any relish of that matter in it which is accounted so acceptable to the 'genus irritabile.' The best answer I can give you is in a clerklike manner to make some observations on two principal points which seem to point like indices into the midst of the whole pro and con about genius and views, and achievements, and ambition et cætera.—1st. As to the poetical Character itself (I mean that sort, of which, if I am anything, I am a member; that sort distinguished from the Wordsworthian, or egotistical Sublime; which is a thing per se, and stands alone,) it is not itself—it has no self—It is everything and nothing—It has no character—it enjoys light and shade; it lives in gusto, be it foul or fair, high or low, rich or poor, mean or elevated—It has as much delight in conceiving an Iago as an Imogen. What shocks the virtuous philosopher delights the chameleon poet. It does no harm from its relish of the dark side of things, any more than from its taste for the bright one, because they both end in speculation. A poet is the most unpoetical of anything in existence, because he has no Identity—he is continually in for and filling some other body. The Sun,—the Moon,—the Sea, and men and women, who are creatures of impulse, are poetical, and have about them an unchangeable attribute; the poet has none, no identity—he is certainly the most unpoetical of all God's creatures.—If then he has no self, and if I am a poet, where is the wonder that I should say I would write no more? Might I not at that very instant have been cogitating on the Characters of Saturn and Ops? It is a wretched thing to confess; but it is a very fact, that not one word I ever utter can be taken for granted as an opinion growing out of my identical Nature—how can it, when I have no Nature? When I am in a room with people, if I ever am free from speculating on creations of my own brain, then, not myself goes home to myself, but the identity of every one in the room begins to press upon me, so that I am in a very little time annihilated— not only among men; it would be the same in a nursery of Children. I know not whether I make myself wholly understood: I hope enough so to let you see that no dependence is to be placed on what I said that day.

In the 2d place, I will speak of my views, and of the life I purpose to myself. I am ambitious of doing the world some good: if I should be spared, that may be the work of maturer years—in the interval I will assay to reach to as high a summit in poetry as the nerve bestowed upon me will suffer. The faint conceptions I have of poems to come bring the blood frequently into my forehead—All I hope is, that I may not lose all interest in human affairs—that the solitary Indifference I feel for applause, even from the finest spirits, will not blunt any acuteness of vision I may have. I do not think it will. I feel assured I should write from the mere yearning and fondness I have for the beautiful, even if my night's labours should be burnt every Morning, and no eye ever shine upon them. But even now I am perhaps not speaking from myself, but from some Character in whose soul I now live.

I am sure however that this next sentence is from myself—
I feel your anxiety, good opinion, and friendship, in the highest
degree, and am

Yours most sincerely

JOHN KEATS

FROM A LETTER TO GEORGE AND GEORGIANA KEATS

February 14–May 3, 1819

. . . The common cognomen of this world among the mis-
guided and superstitious is 'a vale of tears,' from which we are
to be redeemed by a certain arbitrary interposition of God and
taken to Heaven—What a little circumscribed straightened
notion! Call the world if you please 'The vale of Soul-making.'
Then you will find out the use of the world (I am speaking now
in the highest terms for human nature admitting it to be
immortal which I will here take for granted for the purpose
of showing a thought which has struck me concerning it) I say
'Soul-making'—Soul as distinguished from an Intelligence.
There may be intelligences or sparks of the divinity in millions
—but they are not Souls till they acquire identities, till each
one is personally itself. Intelligences are atoms of perception
—they know and they see and they are pure, in short they are
God—how then are the Souls to be made? How then are these
sparks which are God to have identity given them—so as ever
to possess a bliss peculiar to each one's individual existence?
How, but by the medium of a world like this? . . . Do you not
see how necessary a World of Pains and troubles is to school
an Intelligence and make it a soul? . . . Seriously I think it
probable that this system of Soul-making may have been the
Parent of all the more palpable and personal schemes of Re-
demption among the Zoroastrians the Christians and the Hin-

doos. For as one part of the human species must have their carved Jupiter; so another part must have the palpable and named Mediator and Saviour, their Christ, their Oromanes, and their Vishnu. If what I have said should not be plain enough, as I fear it may not be, I will put you in the place where I began in this series of thoughts—I mean I began by seeing how man was formed by circumstances—and what are circumstances but touchstones of his heart? and what are touchstones but provings of his heart, but fortifiers or alterers of his nature? and what is his altered nature but his Soul?— and what was his Soul before it came into the world and had these provings and alterations and perfectionings?—An intelligence without Identity—and how is this Identity to be made? Through the medium of the Heart? and how is the heart to become this Medium but in a world of Circumstances?

There now I think what with Poetry and Theology, you may thank your stars that my pen is not very long-winded. Yesterday I received two Letters from your Mother and Henry, which I shall send by young Birkbeck with this....

II poems of the same period 🌿

The following nine poems are all from the twentieth century. The first group of five happens to contain recurring animal imagery. With what ideas and attitudes is this imagery associated in each poem? Shaped by what context and purpose, and embodied by means of what technical and stylistic devices? Do its uses reveal any similarities in these matters? Can you begin making a few modest generalizations about some facet of modern poetry on this basis?

The second group of four happens to illustrate the use of a similar situation—the moment of transition between night and day. What kind of response does this situation arouse in the speaker of each poem? What ideas and attitudes does it bring to his mind? Are there any similarities among them in these matters? In style, technique, and purpose? Are there any significant similarities between this group and the first group? What do these things tell us about some conventions of modern poetry?

group (a)

THE WOLVES ≪≪- *Allen Tate*

There are wolves in the next room waiting
With heads bent low, thrust out, breathing
At nothing in the dark; between them and me
A white door patched with light from the hall
Where it seems never (so still is the house)
A man has walked from the front door to the stair.
It has all been forever. Beasts claw the floor.
I have brooded on angels and archfiends
But no man has ever sat where the next room's
Crowded with wolves, and for the honor of man
I affirm that never have I before. Now while
I have looked for the evening star at a cold window
And whistled when Arcturus split his light,
I've heard the wolves scuffle, and said: So this
Is man; so—what better conclusion is there—
The day will not follow night, and the heart
Of man has a little dignity, but less patience
Than a wolf's, and a duller sense that cannot
Smell its own mortality. (This and other
Meditations will be suited to other times
After dog silence howls his epitaph.)
Now remember courage, go to the door,
Open it and see whether coiled on the bed
Or cringing by the wall, a savage beast
Maybe with golden hair, with deep eyes
Like a bearded spider on a sunlit floor
Will snarl—and man can never be alone.

ORIGINAL SIN: A SHORT STORY
Robert Penn Warren

Nodding, its great head rattling like a gourd,
And locks like seaweed strung on the stinking stone,
The nightmare stumbles past, and you have heard
It fumble your door before it whimpers and is gone:
It acts like the old hound that used to snuffle your door and
     moan.

You thought you had lost it when you left Omaha,
For it seemed connected then with your grandpa, who
Had a wen on his forehead and sat on the veranda
To finger the precious protuberance, as was his habit to do,
Which glinted in sun like rough garnet or the rich old brain
     bulging through.

But you met it in Harvard Yard as the historic steeple
Was confirming the midnight with its hideous racket,
And you wondered how it had come, for it stood so imbecile,
With empty hands, humble, and surely nothing in pocket:
Riding the rods, perhaps—or grandpa's will paid the ticket.

You were almost kindly then, in your first homesickness,
As it tortured its stiff face to speak, but scarcely mewed;
Since then you have outlived all your homesickness,
But have met it in many another distempered latitude:
Oh, nothing is lost, ever lost! at last you understood.

But it never came in the quantum glare of sun
To shame you before your friends, and had nothing to do
With your public experience or private reformation:
But it thought no bed too narrow—it stood with lips askew
And shook its great head sadly like the abstract Jew.

Never met you in the lyric arsenical meadows
When children call and your heart goes stone in the bosom;
At the orchard anguish never, nor ovoid horror,
Which is furred like a peach or avid like the delicious plum.
It takes no part in your classic prudence or fondled axiom.

Not there when you exclaimed: "Hope is betrayed by
Disastrous glory of sea-capes, sun-torment of whitecaps
—There must be a new innocence for us to be stayed by."
But there it stood, after all the timetables, all the lamps,
In the crepuscular clutter of *always, always,* or *perhaps.*

You have moved often and rarely left an address,
And hear of the deaths of friends with a sly pleasure,
A sense of cleansing and hope, which blooms from distress;
But it has not died, it comes, its hand childish, unsure,
Clutching the bribe of chocolate or a toy you used to treasure.

It tries the lock; you hear, but simply drowse:
There is nothing remarkable in that sound at the door.
Later you hear it wander the dark house
Like a mother who rises at night to seek a childhood picture;
Or it goes to the backyard and stands like an old horse cold
    in the pasture.

THE HEAVY BEAR   ⋘   *Delmore Schwartz*

"the withness of the body"—WHITEHEAD

The heavy bear who goes with me,
A manifold honey to smear his face,
Clumsy and lumbering here and there,
The central ton of every place,

The hungry beating brutish one
In love with candy, anger, and sleep,
Crazy factotum, dishevelling all,
Climbs the building, kicks the football,
Boxes his brother in the hate-ridden city.

Breathing at my side, that heavy animal,
That heavy bear who sleeps with me,
Howls in his sleep for a world of sugar,
A sweetness intimate as the water's clasp,
Howls in his sleep because the tight-rope
Trembles and shows the darkness beneath.
—The strutting show-off is terrified,
Dressed in his dress-suit, bulging his pants,
Trembles to think that his quivering meat
Must finally wince to nothing at all.

That inescapable animal walks with me,
Has followed me since the black womb held,
Moves where I move, distorting my gesture,
A caricature, a swollen shadow,
A stupid clown of the spirit's motive,
Perplexes and affronts with his own darkness,
The secret life of belly and bone,
Opaque, too near, my private, yet unknown,
Stretches to embrace the very dear
With whom I would walk without him near,
Touches her grossly, although a word
Would bare my heart and make me clear,
Stumbles, flounders, and strives to be fed
Dragging me with him in his mouthing care,
Amid the hundred million of his kind,
The scrimmage of appetite everywhere.

A DOG NAMED EGO   ⋘   *Delmore Schwartz*

A dog named Ego, the snowflakes as kisses
Fluttered, ran, came with me in December,
Snuffing the chill air, changing, and halting,
There where I walked toward seven o'clock,
Sniffed at some interests hidden and open,
Whirled, descending, and stood still, attentive,
Seeking their peace, the stranger, unknown,
With me, near me, kissed me, touched my wound,
My simple face, obsessed and pleasure bound.

"Not free, no liberty, rock that you carry,"
So spoke Ego in his cracked and harsh voice,
While snowflakes kissed me and satisfied minutes,
Falling from some place half believed and unknown,
"You will not be free, nor ever alone,"
So spoke Ego, "Mine is the kingdom,
Dynasty's bone: you will not be free,
Go, choose, run, you will not be alone."

"Come, come, come," sang the whirling snowflakes,
Evading the dog who barked at their smallness,
"Come!" sang the snowflakes, "Come here! and here!"
How soon at the sidewalk, melted, and done,
One kissed me, two kissed me! So many died!
While Ego barked at them, swallowed their touch,
Ran this way! And that way! While they slipped to the ground,
Leading him further and farther away,
While night collapsed amid the falling,
And left me no recourse, far from my home,
And left me no recourse, far from my home.

THE GAZABOS ⫷⫷ *Edwin Honig*

I saw them dancing,
the gazabos, apes of joy, swains of
their pocket mirrors, to each a world:
    a dancing, a gallumphing, a guzzling
      of themselves.

They yapped, they cooed,
they flapped their feet and winked grimaces
into grins. They rapped their knuckles on
    their teeth and bled and licked
      the blood like honey.

Turning the corner
to my street, I spat on each
gazabo as they came. They loved it,
    they could barely keep
      from following.

I had to beat
them off with barbed wire switches
ripped from neighbors' fences on
    the way. I escaped
      only when

    they paused to smear
their bodies with their trickly wounds,
streaming welted faces ogle-
    laughing in the mirrors
      sideways.

Why is it now,
safe in my lacquered room, cradled
in my black, spoon-shaped easy
chair, the whitest sheet
of paper on

my knees, I cannot
write a word? I read their eyes,
I taste their wounds. Do they live
because they simply
cannot die?

Friends, multi-
tudes, oh lifelong shadows: are
you my filth, my worn out longings,
my poems that dog me
till I die?

group (b)

THE WAYSIDE STATION ≪← *Edwin Muir*

Here at the wayside station, as many a morning,
I watch the smoke torn from the fumy engine
Crawling across the field in serpent sorrow.
Flat in the east, held down by stolid clouds,
The struggling day is born and shines already
On its warm hearth far off. Yet something here
Glimmers along the ground to show the seagulls
White on the furrows' black unturning waves.

But now the light has broadened.
I watch the farmstead on the little hill,
That seems to mutter: "Here is day again"
Unwillingly. Now the sad cattle wake
In every byre and stall,
The ploughboy stirs in the loft, the farmer groans
And feels the day like a familiar ache
Deep in his body, though the house is dark.
The lovers part
Now in the bedroom where the pillows gleam
Great and mysterious as deep hills of snow,
An inaccessible land. The wood stands waiting
While the bright snare slips coil by coil around it,
Dark silver on every branch. The lonely stream
That rode through darkness leaps the gap of light,
Its voice grown loud, and starts its winding journey
Through the day and time and war and history.

PRIME ⋘ *W. H. Auden*

FROM *Horae Canonicae*

Simultaneously, as soundlessly,
  Spontaneously, suddenly
As, at the vaunt of the dawn, the kind
  Gates of the body fly open
To its world beyond, the gates of the mind,
  The horn gate and the ivory gate
Swing to, swing shut, instantaneously
  Quell the nocturnal rummage
Of its rebellious fronde, ill-favored,
  Ill-natured and second-rate,

Disenfranchised, widowed and orphaned
  By an historical mistake:
Recalled from the shades to be a seeing being,
  From absence to be on display,
Without a name or history I wake
  Between my body and the day.

Holy this moment, wholly in the right,
  As, in complete obedience
To the light's laconic outcry, next
  As a sheet, near as a wall,
Out there as a mountain's poise of stone,
  The world is present, about,
And I know that I am, here, not alone
  But with a world and rejoice
Unvexed, for the will has still to claim
  This adjacent arm as my own,
The memory to name me, resume
  Its routine of praise and blame
And smiling to me is this instant while
  Still the day is intact, and I
The Adam sinless in our beginning,
  Adam still previous to any act.

I draw breath; this is of course to wish
  No matter what, to be wise,
To be different, to die and the cost,
  No matter how, is Paradise
Lost of course and myself owing a death:
  The eager ridge, the steady sea,
The flat roofs of the fishing village
  Still asleep in its bunny.
Though as fresh and sunny still are not friends
  But things to hand, this ready flesh

No honest equal, but my accomplice now
  My assassin to be, and my name
Stands for my historical share of care
  For a lying self-made city,
Afraid of our living task, the dying
  Which the coming day will ask.

IN THE NAKED BED, IN PLATO'S CAVE 《《←
Delmore Schwartz

In the naked bed, in Plato's cave,
Reflected headlights slowly slid the wall,
Carpenters hammered under the shaded window,
Wind troubled the window curtains all night long,
A fleet of trucks strained uphill, grinding,
Their freights covered, as usual.
The ceiling lightened again, the slanting diagram
Slid slowly forth.
                    Hearing the milkman's chop,
His striving up the stair, the bottle's chink,
I rose from bed, lit a cigarette,
And walked to the window. The stony street
Displayed the stillness in which buildings stand,
The street-lamp's vigil and the horse's patience.
The winter sky's pure capital
Turned me back to bed with exhausted eyes.

Strangeness grew in the motionless air. The loose
Film grayed. Shaking wagons, hooves' waterfalls,
Sounded far off, increasing, louder and nearer.
A car coughed, starting. Morning, softly
Melting the air, lifted the half-covered chair
From underseas, kindled the looking-glass,

Distinguished the dresser and the white wall.
The bird called tentatively, whistled, called,
Bubbled and whistled, so! Perplexed, still wet
With sleep, affectionate, hungry and cold. So, so,
O son of man, the ignorant night, the travail
Of early morning, the mystery of beginning
Again and again,
              while History is unforgiven.

LOVE CALLS US TO THE THINGS OF THIS WORLD ⋘ *Richard Wilbur*

The eyes open to a cry of pulleys,
And spirited from sleep, the astounded soul
Hangs for a moment bodiless and simple
As false dawn.
            Outside the open window
The morning air is all awash with angels.

Some are in bed-sheets, some are in blouses,
Some are in smocks: but truly there they are.
Now they are rising together in calm swells
Of halcyon feeling, filling whatever they wear
With the deep joy of their impersonal breathing;

Now they are flying in place, conveying
The terrible speed of their omnipresence, moving
And staying like white water; and now of a sudden
They swoon down into so rapt a quiet
That nobody seems to be there.
                The soul shrinks

From all that it is about to remember,
From the punctual rape of every blessèd day,
And cries,
         "Oh, let there be nothing on earth but laundry,
Nothing but rosy hands in the rising steam
And clear dances done in the sight of heaven."

         Yet, as the sun acknowledges
With a warm look the world's hunks and colors,
The soul descends once more in bitter love
To accept the waking body, saying now
In a changed voice as the man yawns and rises,

         "Bring them down from their ruddy gallows;
Let there be clean linen for the backs of thieves;
Let lovers go fresh and sweet to be undone,
And the heaviest nuns walk in a pure floating
Of dark habits,
             keeping their difficult balance."

III poems of different periods

The following group of six poems is arranged chronologically, with each poem drawn from one of the major English literary periods. As suggested in the Appendix, they are all built around a similar poetic context. What changes in the handling of a similar structure do you notice from period to period regarding diction, situation, attitudes, and ideas, the character of the speaker, the nature of the conclusion, the techniques, and so on? What aspects of each poem seem to be primarily governed by the formal requirements of the poem itself, what by the vision and temperament of the poet, and what by the pressures of the period? Here the aim is to acquire a sense of the changing characteristics of the poetic art from period to period, of what typifies each age and the sequence by which changes come about.

the sixteenth century

SONNET LXV   ⋘ *William Shakespeare*

Since brass, nor stone, nor earth, nor boundless sea,
But sad mortality o'er-sways their power,
How with this rage shall beauty hold a plea,
Whose action is no stronger than a flower?
O, how shall summer's honey breath hold out
Against the wreckful siege of battering days,
When rocks impregnable are not so stout,
Nor gates of steel so strong, but Time decays?
O fearful meditation! Where, alack,
Shall Time's best jewel from Time's chest lie hid?
Or what strong hand can hold his swift foot back,
Or who his spoil of beauty can forbid?
   O, none, unless this miracle have might,
    That in black ink my love may still shine bright.
[*1593–1600*]

the seventeenth century

LYCIDAS ⫷⫸ *John Milton*

A LAMENT FOR A FRIEND DROWNED IN HIS PASSAGE FROM CHESTER
ON THE IRISH SEAS, 1637

Yet once more, O ye Laurels, and once more
Ye Myrtles brown, with Ivy never sere,
I com to pluck your Berries harsh and crude,
And with forc't fingers rude
Shatter your leaves before the mellowing year.
Bitter constraint, and sad occasion dear,
Compels me to disturb your season due;
For *Lycidas* is dead, dead ere his prime,
Young *Lycidas*, and hath not left his peer.
Who would not sing for *Lycidas?* he knew
Himself to sing, and build the lofty rhyme.
He must not flote upon his wat'ry bear
Unwept, and welter to the parching wind,
Without the meed of some melodious tear.
　Begin, then, Sisters of the sacred well
That from beneath the seat of *Jove* doth spring,
Begin, and somewhat loudly sweep the string.
Hence with denial vain, and coy excuse;
So may som gentle Muse
With lucky words favor my destin'd Urn,
And as he passes turn,
And bid fair peace be to my sable shroud.
For we were neerst upon the self-same hill,
Fed the same flock, by fountain, shade, and rill.
　Together both, ere the high Lawns appear'd
Under the opening eyelids of the morn,

We drove afield, and both together heard
What time the Gray-fly winds her sultry horn,
Batt'ning our flocks with the fresh dews of night,
Oft till the Star that rose, at Ev'ning, bright
Toward Heav'ns descent had slop'd his westering wheel
Meanwhile the Rural ditties were not mute,
Tempered to th' Oaten Flute;
Rough *Satyrs* danced, and *Fauns* with clov'n heel
From the glad sound would not be absent long,
And old *Damœtas* loved to hear our song.

But O the heavy change, now thou art gone,
Now thou art gone, and never must return!
Thee, Shepherd, thee the Woods and desert Caves,
With wild Thyme and the gadding Vine o'ergrown,
And all their echoes mourn.
The Willows and the Hazel Copses green
Shall now no more be seen
Fanning their joyous Leaves to thy soft lays.
As killing as the Canker to the Rose,
Or taint-worm to the weanling Herds that graze,
Or Frost to Flowers, that their gay wardrop wear,
When first the White thorn blows;
Such, *Lycidas*, thy loss to Shepherds ear.

Where were ye, Nymphs, when the remorseless deep
Closed o'er the head of your lov'd *Lycidas?*
For neither were ye playing on the steep
Where your old *Bards*, the famous *Druids*, ly,
Nor on the shaggy top of *Mona* high,
Nor yet where *Deva* spreads her wizard stream.
Ay me, I fondly dream,
Had ye bin there!—for what could that have done?
What could the Muse herself that Orpheus bore,
The Muse herself, for her enchanting son,

Whom Universal Nature did lament,
When by the rout that made the hideous roar
His goary visage down the stream was sent,
Down the swift *Hebrus* to the *Lesbian* shore?
  Alas! what boots it with uncessant care
To tend the homely slighted Shepherds trade,
And strictly meditate the thankles Muse?
Were it not better done as others use,
To sport with *Amaryllis* in the shade,
Or with the tangles of *Neaera's* hair?
Fame is the spur that the clear spirit doth raise
(That last infirmity of Noble mind)
To scorn delights, and live laborious days;
But the fair Guerdon when we hope to find,
And think to burst out into sudden blaze,
Comes the blind *Fury* with th' abhorred shears,
And slits the thin spun life. But not the praise,
Phoebus replid, and touched my trembling ears:
Fame is no plant that grows on mortal soil,
Nor in the glistering foil
Set off to th' world, nor in broad rumour lies,
But lives and spreds aloft by those pure eyes
And perfect witness of all-judging *Jove*;
As he pronounces lastly on each deed,
Of so much fame in Heav'n expect thy meed.
  O fountain *Arethuse*, and thou honour'd floud,
Smooth-sliding *Mincius*, crowned with vocall reeds,
That strain I heard was of a higher mood.
But now my Oat proceeds,
And listens to the Herald of the Sea,
That came in *Neptune's* plea.
He ask'd the waves, and ask'd the Fellon winds,
What hard mishap hath doomed this gentle swain?
And question'd every gust of rugged wings

That blows from off each beaked Promontory;
They knew not of his story,
And sage *Hippotades* their answer brings,
That not a blast was from his dungeon stray'd;
The Ayr was calm, and on the level brine
Sleek *Panope* with all her sisters play'd.
It was that fatall and perfidious Bark,
Built in th' eclipse, and rigg'd with curses dark,
That sunk so low that sacred head of thine.

   Next *Camus*, reverend Sire, went footing slow,
His Mantle hairy, and his Bonnet sedge,
Inwrought with figures dim, and on the edge
Like to that sanguine flower inscribed with woe.
Ah, who hath reft, (quoth he) my dearest pledge?
Last came, and last did go,
The Pilot of the *Galilean* Lake;
Two massy Keyes he bore of metals twain
(The Golden opes, the Iron shuts amain).
He shook his Miter'd locks, and stern bespake:
How well could I have spared for thee, young swain,
Anow of such as for their bellies sake,
Creep and intrude and climb into the fold?
Of other care they little reck'ning make
Than how to scramble at the shearers feast,
And shove away the worthy bidden guest.
Blind mouthes! that scarce themselves know how to hold
A Sheep-hook, or have learn'd aught els the least
That to the faithfull Herdmans art belongs!
What recks it them? What need they? They are sped;
And when they list, their lean and flashy songs
Grate on their scrannel Pipes of wretched straw;
The hungry sheep look up, and are not fed,
But swoln with wind and the rank mist they draw,
Rot inwardly, and foul contagion spread;

Besides what the grim Woolf with privy paw
Daily devours apace, and nothing said;
But that two-handed engine at the door
Stands ready to smite once, and smite no more.
    Return, *Alpheus*, the dread voice is past
That shrunk thy streams; return, *Sicilian* Muse,
And call the Vales, and bid them hither cast
Their Bels and Flourets of a thousand hues.
Ye valleys low where the milde whispers use
Of shades and wanton winds and gushing brooks,
On whose fresh lap the swart Star sparely looks,
Throw hither all your quaint enameld eyes,
That on the green terf suck the honied showres,
And purple all the ground with vernal flowres.
Bring the rathe Primrose that forsaken dies,
The tufted Crow-toe, and pale Gessamine,
The white Pink, and the Pansie freakt with jeat,
The glowing Violet.
The Musk-rose, and the well-attir'd Woodbine,
With Cowslips wan that hang the pensive hed,
And every flower that sad embroidery wears:
Bid *Amaranthus* all his beauty shed,
And Daffadillies fill their cups with tears,
To strew the Laureate herse where *Lycid* lies.
For so to interpose a little ease,
Let our frail thoughts dally with false surmise;
Ay me! whilst thee the shores and sounding Seas
Washed far away, where'er thy bones are hurld,
Whether beyond the stormy *Hebrides*,
Where thou perhaps under the whelming tide
Visit'st the bottom of the monstrous world;
Or whether thou, to our moist vows deny'd,
Sleep'st by the fable of *Bellerus* old,
Where the great vision of the guarded Mount

Looks toward *Namancos* and *Bayona's* hold;
Look homeward Angel now, and melt with ruth,
And, O ye *Dolphins*, waft the haples youth.
    Weep no more, woful Shepherds, weep no more,
For *Lycidas*, your sorrow, is not dead,
Sunk though he be beneath the watry floar;
So sinks the day-star in the Ocean bed,
And yet anon repairs his drooping head,
And tricks his beams, and with new spangled Ore
Flames in the forehead of the morning sky:
So *Lycidas* sunk low, but mounted high,
Through the dear might of him that walkd the waves,
Where, other groves and other streams along,
With *Nectar* pure his oozy Locks he laves,
And hears the unexpressive nuptiall Song,
In the blest Kingdoms meek of joy and love.
There entertain him all the Saints above,
In solemn troops and sweet Societies
That sing, and singing in their glory move,
And wipe the tears for ever from his eyes.
Now, *Lycidas*, the Shepherds weep no more;
Henceforth thou art the Genius of the shore,
In thy large recompense, and shalt be good
To all that wander in that perilous flood.
    Thus sang the uncouth Swain to th' Okes and rills,
While the still morn went out with Sandals gray,
He touch'd the tender stops of various Quills,
With eager thought warbling his *Dorick* lay:
And now the Sun had stretchd out all the hills,
And now was dropt into the Western bay;
At last he rose, and twitchd his Mantle blew:
To-morrow to fresh Woods, and Pastures new.
[*1637*]

ELEGY WRITTEN IN A COUNTRY CHURCHYARD ⫷ *Thomas Gray*

The Curfew tolls the knell of parting day,
The lowing herd wind slowly o'er the lea,
The plowman homeward plods his weary way,
And leaves the world to darkness and to me.

Now fades the glimmering landscape on the sight,
And all the air a solemn stillness holds,
Save where the beetle wheels his droning flight,
And drowsy tinklings lull the distant folds;

Save that from yonder ivy-mantled tow'r
The mopeing owl does to the moon complain
Of such, as wand'ring near her secret bow'r,
Molest her ancient solitary reign.

Beneath those rugged elms, that yew-tree's shade,
Where heaves the turf in many a mould'ring heap,
Each in his narrow cell for ever laid,
The rude Forefathers of the hamlet sleep.

The breezy call of incense-breathing Morn,
The swallow twitt'ring from the straw-built shed,
The cock's shrill clarion, or the echoing horn,
No more shall rouse them from their lowly bed.

For them no more the blazing hearth shall burn,
Or busy housewife ply her evening care:
No children run to lisp their sire's return,
Or climb his knees the envied kiss to share.

Oft did the harvest to their sickle yield,
Their furrow oft the stubborn glebe has broke;
How jocund did they drive their team afield!
How bow'd the woods beneath their sturdy stroke!

Let not Ambition mock their useful toil,
Their homely joys, and destiny obscure;
Nor Grandeur hear with a disdainful smile,
The short and simple annals of the poor.

The boast of heraldry, the pomp of pow'r,
And all that beauty, all that wealth e'er gave,
Awaits alike th' inevitable hour.
The paths of glory lead but to the grave.

Nor you, ye Proud, impute to These the fault,
If Mem'ry o'er their Tomb no Trophies raise,
Where thro' the long-drawn isle and fretted vault
The pealing anthem swells the note of praise.

Can storied urn or animated bust
Back to its mansion call the fleeting breath?
Can Honour's voice provoke the silent dust,
Or Flatt'ry sooth the dull cold ear of Death?

Perhaps in this neglected spot is laid
Some heart once pregnant with celestial fire;
Hands, that the rod of empire might have sway'd,
Or wak'd to extasy the living lyre.

But Knowledge to their eyes her ample page
Rich with the spoils of time did ne'er unroll;
Chill Penury repress'd their noble rage,
And froze the genial current of the soul.

Full many a gem of purest ray serene,
The dark unfathom'd caves of ocean bear:
Full many a flower is born to blush unseen,
And waste its sweetness on the desert air.

Some village-Hampden, that with dauntless breast
The little Tyrant of his fields withstood;
Some mute inglorious Milton here may rest,
Some Cromwell guiltless of his country's blood.

Th' applause of list'ning senates to command,
The threats of pain and ruin to despise,
To scatter plenty o'er a smiling land,
And read their hist'ry in a nation's eyes,

Their lot forbad: nor circumscrib'd alone
Their growing virtues, but their crimes confin'd;
Forbad to wade through slaughter to a throne,
And shut the gates of mercy on mankind,

The struggling pangs of conscious truth to hide,
To quench the blushes of ingenuous shame,
Or heap the shrine of Luxury and Pride
With incense kindled at the Muse's flame.

Far from the madding crowd's ignoble strife,
Their sober wishes never learn'd to stray;
Along the cool sequester'd vale of life
They kept the noiseless tenor of their way.

Yet ev'n these bones from insult to protect
Some frail memorial still erected nigh,
With uncouth rhimes and shapeless sculpture deck'd,
Implores the passing tribute of a sigh.

Their name, their years, spelt by th' unletter'd muse,
The place of fame and elegy supply:
And many a holy text around she strews,
That teach the rustic moralist to die.

For who to dumb Forgetfulness a prey,
This pleasing anxious being e'er resign'd,
Left the warm precincts of the chearful day,
Nor cast one longing ling'ring look behind?

On some fond breast the parting soul relies,
Some pious drops the closing eye requires;
Ev'n from the tomb the voice of Nature cries,
Ev'n in our Ashes live their wonted Fires.

For thee, who mindful of th' unhonour'd Dead
Dost in these lines their artless tale relate;
If chance, by lonely contemplation led,
Some kindred Spirit shall inquire thy fate,

Haply some hoary-headed Swain may say,
'Oft have we seen him at the peep of dawn
'Brushing with hasty steps the dews away
'To meet the sun upon the upland lawn.

'There at the foot of yonder nodding beech
'That wreathes its old fantastic roots so high,
'His listless length at noontide would he stretch,
'And pore upon the brook that babbles by.

'Hard by yon wood, now smiling as in scorn,
'Mutt'ring his wayward fancies he would rove,
'Now drooping, woeful wan, like one forlorn,
'Or craz'd with care, or cross'd in hopeless love.

'One morn I miss'd him on the custom'd hill,
'Along the heath and near his fav'rite tree;
'Another came; nor yet beside the rill,
'Nor up the lawn, nor at the wood was he;

'The next with dirges due in sad array
'Slow thro' the church-way path we saw him born.
'Approach and read (for thou can'st read) the lay,
'Grav'd on the stone beneath yon aged thorn.'

The Epitaph

Here rests his head upon the lap of Earth
A Youth to Fortune and to Fame unknown.
Fair Science frown'd not on his humble birth,
And Melancholy mark'd him for her own.

Large was his bounty, and his soul sincere,
Heav'n did a recompence as largely send:
He gave to Mis'ry all he had, a tear,
He gain'd from Heav'n ('twas all he wish'd) a friend.

No farther seek his merits to disclose,
Or draw his frailties from their dread abode,
(There they alike in trembling hope repose,)
The bosom of his Father and his God.

the nineteenth century: romantic

ODE ON A GRECIAN URN ⋘ *John Keats*

I

Thou still unravish'd bride of quietness,
  Thou foster-child of silence and slow time,
Sylvan historian, who canst thus express
  A flowery tale more sweetly than our rhyme:
What leaf-fring'd legend haunts about thy shape
  Of deities or mortals, or of both,
    In Tempe or the dales of Arcady?
  What men or gods are these? What maidens loth?
What mad pursuit? What struggle to escape?
    What pipes and timbrels? What wild ecstasy?

II

Heard melodies are sweet, but those unheard
  Are sweeter; therefore, ye soft pipes, play on;
Not to the sensual ear, but, more endear'd,
  Pipe to the spirit ditties of no tone:
Fair youth, beneath the trees, thou canst not leave
  Thy song, nor ever can those trees be bare;
    Bold lover, never, never canst thou kiss,
Though winning near the goal—yet, do not grieve;
    She cannot fade, though thou hast not thy bliss,
  For ever wilt thou love, and she be fair!

III

Ah, happy, happy boughs! that cannot shed
  Your leaves, nor ever bid the Spring adieu;
And, happy melodist, unwearied,

For ever piping songs for ever new;
More happy love! more happy, happy love!
For ever warm and still to be enjoy'd,
    For ever panting, and for ever young;
All breathing human passion far above,
        That leaves a heart high-sorrowful and cloy'd,
            A burning forehead, and a parching tongue.

IV

Who are these coming to the sacrifice?
    To what green altar, O mysterious priest,
Lead'st thou that heifer lowing at the skies,
    And all her silken flanks with garlands drest?
What little town by river or sea shore,
    Or mountain-built with peaceful citadel,
        Is emptied of its folk, this pious morn?
And, little town, thy streets for evermore
        Will silent be; and not a soul to tell
            Why thou art desolate, can e'er return.

V

O Attic shape! Fair attitude! with brede
    Of marble men and maidens overwrought,
With forest branches and the trodden weed;
    Thou, silent form, dost tease us out of thought
As doth eternity: Cold Pastoral!
    When old age shall this generation waste,
        Thou shalt remain, in midst of other woe
        Than ours, a friend to man, to whom thou say'st,
"Beauty is truth, truth beauty,"—that is all
        Ye know on earth, and all ye need to know.
    [*1819*]

the nineteenth century: victorian

DOVER BEACH ⫷ *Matthew Arnold*

The sea is calm tonight.
The tide is full, the moon lies fair
Upon the straits;—on the French coast the light
Gleams and is gone; the cliffs of England stand,
Glimmering and vast, out in the tranquil bay.
Come to the window, sweet is the night air!

Only, from the long line of spray
Where the sea meets the moon-blanched land,
Listen! you hear the grating roar
Of pebbles which the waves draw back, and fling,
At their return, up the high strand,
Begin, and cease, and then again begin,
With tremulous cadence slow, and bring
The eternal note of sadness in.

Sophocles long ago
Heard it on the Aegean, and it brought
Into his mind the turbid ebb and flow
Of human misery; we
Find also in the sound a thought,
Hearing it by this distant northern sea.

The Sea of Faith
Was once, too, at the full, and round earth's shore
Lay like the folds of a bright girdle furled.
But now I only hear

Its melancholy, long, withdrawing roar,
Retreating, to the breath
Of the night wind, down the vast edges drear
And naked shingles of the world.

Ah, love, let us be true
To one another! for the world, which seems
To lie before us like a land of dreams,
So various, so beautiful, so new,
Hath really neither joy, nor love, nor light,
Nor certitude, nor peace, nor help for pain;
And we are here as on a darkling plain
Swept with confused alarms of struggle and flight,
Where ignorant armies clash by night.
[*1867*]

the twentieth century

SAILING TO BYZANTIUM ⫷⫷⫷
William Butler Yeats

I

That is no country for old men. The young
In one another's arms, birds in the trees,
—Those dying generations—at their song,
The salmon-falls, the mackerel-crowded seas,
Fish, flesh, or fowl, commend all summer long
Whatever is begotten, born, and dies.
Caught in that sensual music all neglect
Monuments of unageing intellect.

II

An aged man is but a paltry thing,
A tattered coat upon a stick, unless
Soul clap its hands and sing, and louder sing
For every tatter in its mortal dress,
Nor is there singing school but studying
Monuments of its own magnificence;
And therefore I have sailed the seas and come
To the holy city of Byzantium.

III

O sages standing in God's holy fire
As in the gold mosaic of a wall,
Come from the holy fire, perne in a gyre,
And be the singing-masters of my soul.
Consume my heart away; sick with desire
And fastened to a dying animal

It knows not what it is; and gather me
Into the artifice of eternity.

IV

Once out of nature I shall never take
My bodily form from any natural thing,
But such a form as Grecian goldsmiths make
Of hammered gold and gold enamelling
To keep a drowsy Emperor awake;
Or set upon a golden bough to sing
To lords and ladies of Byzantium
Of what is past, or passing, or to come.
[*1928*]

index of terms

247

index of poems by author